Almost Heaven

L E S L I E
T H O M A S

Almost Heaven

TRUE and ALMOST TRUE TALES
ABOUT A CATHEDRAL

Bene Factum Publishing Ltd

For my dear grand-daughter Zoë Elizabeth Thomas who was christened in Salisbury Cathedral and for my newly-born grandson, Vincent Leslie Randolph Thomas who will be christened there.

First published in 2010
by Bene Factum Publishing Ltd
PO Box 58122
London
SW8 5WZ

Email: inquiries@bene-factum.co.uk
www.bene-factum.co.uk

ISBN: 978-1-903071-23-6

A CIP catalogue record of this is available from the British Library

Design and Typesetting by Ian Hughes – Mousemat Design Limited
Printed and bound by Clays Ltd, St Ives Group, UK

Author's Note

TALES ARE TALES. THEY COME in all shapes and guises, ancient and modern (which does not necessarily guarantee authenticity).

Here are stories, part history, part anecdote, part legend, with sometimes a good pinch of truth. Some are not necessarily based on a deep foundation – rather like Salisbury Cathedral itself. But, like the Cathedral, they still stand.

This is a collection of such tales – stories not only from the Cathedral but its Close, its adjoining habitations, and its river-fringed meadows – the places *ABOUT* it.

Leslie Thomas
Salisbury. 2010

Contents

"... Wandering one midsummer evening
round the purlieus of Salisbury Cathedral ..."

Anthony Trollope 1882
on the inspiration behind his "Barchester" Novels.

CHAPTER I

Close Quarters

A FEW FEET BELOW THE peak of the tallest cathedral spire in Britain sits a pensive peregrine falcon apparently taking in the view. Sometimes he shows himself although only remotely, but those who have climbed the bracing four hundred feet of tenuous steps have found clues – a rabbit skin, a pair of gutted pigeons, a lost cat never to be found.

A man called Old Halley once sat up there and ate his dinner, every mouthful cheered by the townspeople of Salisbury far below. Halley and the falcon, two early cases of *haute cuisine*. Halley, not a steeplejack but a plumber, perhaps ate his meal by torchlight, although his picnic of a leg of mutton and "two fowles" cannot have been easily transported. I enjoy thinking of the falcon, dining on a fading summer evening, spread before him not only a decent meal but a view without equal in domestic England.

Salisbury Cathedral Close is a green lagoon with its houses encircling like islands; ancient places of different coloured roofs and walls, haunted by history, famous and often eccentric characters, and any number of ghosts. Eighty three acres, where people lie on the summer grass that lies over a graveyard; children skip, youths play football, although the latter is not allowed. They stop when the watchman of The Close admonishes them but then continue their hoofing once he has returned to his house or his duty cubby hole. It was so back through history, although these days there are more people but fewer murders.

It is a holy place but it lives for every day. You can even get a glass of wine (or several) in the Cathedral Refectory. Some way back they had to demolish the bell tower because of drunkenness, the presence of unsuitable women and hooligans who "jambled the bells".

Whichever road you take to Salisbury the Cathedral can be seen from far off. The city is built in a saucer and the spire stands upright like a candle in a holder.

Driving down the route that was old before the Romans came, from the direction of Stockbridge and – eighty miles or so beyond that – London, you turn a sudden bend in the countryside and there, in the distance, mixed with mist, dulled with cloud or pinpointed by the sun, but always there, is the spire.

Come from Southampton and the sea, and from the rise of Pepperbox Hill, known to Dickens, it pierces the landscape ahead; from Thomas Hardy's Wessex it rises as the road falls. Hardy himself used to love to cycle from Dorchester to Salisbury for Evensong and in his search for answers.

To the South the way emerges from under the boughs of the New Forest trees and there is the spire like a signpost; it can be seen too as you travel over the hump of Salisbury Plain, where buzzards circle and hares run, often prompted by army gunfire. The switchback road skirts the blancmange shape of the fortress and holy hill of Old Sarum where this story started.

Whichever way we came we, Diana and I, and assorted children, always watched for the first glimpse of the far-off spire and when we saw it we would be singing out in adopted wurzle Wessex voices: "Thur She Be!"

And there she always was, guiding us home. The route fell through the everyday countryside of the Ancient Britons, eventually levelling as we reached the city of Salisbury. It has changed, obviously, but not so much as most places, the old prints and drawings still fit the streets with their quirky names, Pennyfarthing Street, Endless Street and Oatmeal Row. Regrettably Milk Monger Street has been renamed.

Then, under the crouching arch, one side holding up the other and into the fastness of The Close, the duty constable sitting in his box like a bulldog in a kennel. He would recognise the car and give thumbs up for us to proceed, or perhaps indicating that nothing had gone amiss, there were no alarums, that nothing had changed since we had been absent. We were home.

Over the years Salisbury has had some colourful clergy and something like a tradition of odd organists. One was unseated from his previous organ stool at Gloucester Cathedral because during pauses between the sacred music he would play the pop tunes of the day and ladies in the congregation would get up from their pews and begin to dance.

Another, William Powell, who held a position as a singing vicar was a drunk, and something of an all-round villain. After a series of fights and misdemeanours he was somehow allowed to take part in an ecclesiastical hare-shoot on Salisbury Plain. He was the worse-for-wear when he arrived, although it was early morning, and had a stand-up fight with one of the beaters. The beater, true to his job description, returned the attack and ended the incident by flooring the cleric with a *dead hare*.

The clergy often seemed to have their minds elsewhere. One Dean, coming into the Cathedral from the rain, brought up the rear of the procession and paced solemnly to the chancel with his dripping umbrella remaining open over him. Another, struggling with a high note, dropped his teeth in front of the high altar. At a more recent service an amplifier behind the altar was inadvertently left active and a burst of blue language came from there to puncture the Te Deum.

Characters in The Close and the Cathedral were outraged when Anthony Trollope wrote his Barchester Towers and the following novels in which, they protested, some of the figures were based on them; perhaps a case of "if the cap fits". But although Trollope had admitted that the notion to write a churchy story came to him one evening as he wandered in the "purlieus of Salisbury Cathedral" he always maintained that Mrs.

Proudie and his other odd characters were based on the denizens of the Close at Winchester. Few Salisbury residents believed him.

On one of our first Sundays living in our house - a Georgian Canonry – in The Close at Salisbury, however, a figure only Trollope could have imagined came into our garden by the river.

It was a spring day, soft and sunny, and we had enjoyed listening to the choirboy voices coming from the morning service over the grass and the trees. Then he appeared, uninvited, loping around the flank of the house, a beaming, bouncy figure in a clerical coat "It's Barchester!" he exclaimed happily. "It's Barchester!"

Trollope may have argued the point but I agreed it was very like it. His name was Canon John Kerruish, a merry Manxman. He became our first friend. He was convinced that Trollope had made some mistake or was merely shifting geography to get people off his back. He was the happiest of canons and we enjoyed visiting him in his tucked away home. Old maps, Speed, Morden and Ogilby, decorated the passage. John Ogilby had been dancing master to the King and perceived the Waywizer maps, showing the curling English roads that helped to open up the country to travellers after The Civil War. Canon Kerruish showed us a cupboard in which was jammed, just, a bed. "The guest suite," he said.

The delight of his life was his Oxford College – Magdalen. He knew every footnote of its history, who had been there and when. Each week he would make a one day pilgrimage by rail, dining at the high table, and returning by the last train of the day. The Salisbury station staff knew him well and after he had alighted, with a beaming face and sometimes with difficulty, onto the platform they knew they could shut up for the night.

When he became ill I used to see him trying to beat his illness by jogging. I was playing cricket one evening for the Gentlemen of The Close when he puffed chubbily by, thick in an ancient jersey and singing something that might have been a hymn. "Barchester!" he croaked as he saw me at deep square leg. "Barchester."

Dying clergy in the past had sometimes, when they could rise to it, sung for the final time as they passed away but John Kerruish bettered this. When he died in Salisbury Hospital he had the choir from his beloved Magdalen College ranged about his bed, hymning him into Heaven. Whether he joined in I do not know. He would have certainly tried.

Our house had been occupied by a large (ten children), talented and endearingly eccentric family. Every child was beautiful and every one musical. There was a whole cupboard full of discarded violins and in a basement was an organ which they had somehow overlooked and which remained there during our ten year tenure. The alluring daughters had been known to wade into the river, wearing airy nighties, flinging tidbits to the enchanted swans while singing pretty songs or reciting Shakespeare. When their father, a Peer, returned to Salisbury Station after a hard day debating in the House of Lords, two of the children would take a dinghy upriver and his lordship would clamber over the gunwale to journey home in style.

Sometimes on a serene evening, Diana and I would walk down the long lawn we had laid to a bench on the bank of the river. The water was the colour of a white wine bottle; it waved into reeds, and there were indolent fish rolling their eyes among the roots of a willow. From the far bank water meadows spread, misty as the sun fell, the territory of various animals and birds and occasional poachers. A prosperous looking fox, auburn coat, showy tail, and proud ears, would often come and sit directly opposite, having a wash, as we drank our gin and tonics. He looked at us and we looked at him. Nobody said anything. Eventually he would up and trot off to find his unsuspecting supper and we would leave too, our fine house standing brick red at the top of the lawn.

Neither of us had been born to this. I had eventually arrived here from a council house in South Wales and my wife was born in a Leicester terrace. It was not difficult to wonder how we had got to The Walton Canonry.

Edward Heath, the most famous man in The Close, was the first to ask us to lunch. He lived two hundred yards down the street. Looking out from his window to the Cathedral I said honestly: "I don't know how I came to live here. I am a working class boy".

Ted said: "So am I".

CHAPTER 2

Once Upon a Hill

E VEN ON A GOOD MORNING in late spring, with a pale sky reaching visibly from Dorset to Hampshire the hill at Old Sarum is an oddly discomfiting place. All around the meadows of May beam amiably but up there it is a different country, the wind niggles in the shabby grass and it only needs a small travelling cloud to make it wintry. No birds sing although I thought I heard from somewhere far below the chimes of an ice-cream van.

In the Salisbury Cloisters today there is a bold model of Old Sarum as it would have once looked. Sometimes I go for morning tea and a home-baked chocolate brownie in the Cathedral refectory and each time I pause and take in another aspect of the glass-cased model, the Norman keep, sturdy as a drum, the surrounding dwellings, more like hovels I imagine in those days, all within the hoop of the castle wall.

Down below, set aside from the castle as if on a shelf, the shape of the original Old Sarum Cathedral stands.

The view today is a stark outline of the ancient church spread out in neat geometric lines, the sort of aspect a pilot gets when taking his plane into an airport. From the toothy battlements of the keep the soldiers could look out for miles until, their watch finished, then find some comfort in their quarters. It was not a bad posting; but no place for a windy church.

But this unpromising site is where Salisbury was conceived and born. Timeless tribes lived on the hill where they could see predators approaching; then the Saxons came and the Romans and eventually William the Conqueror's Normans. It was given a litany of names – Searobyrg, Sorviodunum and eventually the faintly recognisable Sarisberie.

The Romans used well-worn tracks as the hard-core of their roads and these converged on a place where there was a ford across the Wessex Avon. It is called Stratford-sub-Castle and it remains there today, occasionally sought out by uncareful tourists who in error put two and two together – Stratford and Avon – and then search diligently for Shakespeare's house. It is a working village however; our local builder has his yard there.

When the Danes, with their usual savage workmanship, began pillaging the surrounding countryside, the people from Wilton and small Wessex villages prudently headed for the sanctuary of the Old Sarum fortress and, in the end, perhaps thinking, with the frequency of the raids, that it was scarcely worth going home, some of them stayed.

Bishop Osmund, who later became Saint Osmund, although he had to wait 350 years for that distinction, built the original Cathedral. He was a truly saintly man, and clever too, widely travelled and educated. But on this bleak and unpopular location he seems to have made one of the few mistakes of his life. The monks moaned almost as much as the wind. Cold and comfortless they complained, and so exposed to the wind that they could scarcely hear themselves chant. Their prayers were carried away by the weather, they suffered rheumatics and pneumonia. There was a groan for every season; even in summer the stark limestone of the hill damaged their eyes. No skylarks sang. They did not like the place.

Nor did the occupying soldiers like them being there. They spitefully fixed the lid on the castle well so that the monks had to carry their water in pots and goatskins up the rough hill; when the soldiers came in drunk from the night-time taverns they made sure their oaths carried to the monks who were trying to get to sleep before getting up at three o'clock to pray. And the monks made sure they sang lustily while facing the direction of the sleeping troops.

Frequently even the bishop found the castle gate locked against him. There were what one scribe noted as "brawls and saddle-blowes", the unarmed but disgruntled monks often giving as good as they got.

The catalyst to this glum situation occurred when a religious procession at Rogation-tide, the three holy days before Ascension, was mumbling up the slope to the main gate and had to halt because the commander of the guard refused to unbolt the door. For several hours apparently. It was a state of things that could not go on.

As it happened, Bishop Poore, a little further along the ecclesiastical succession, belied his name by owning a wonderfully verdant stretch of land, held in the bend of a curling river, and less than an hour's walk away. The Pope had to give his consent for the monks to move and, since he did not live at Old Sarum and Rome was half-way around the world, he took some years. But eventually the message came. The freezing friars could move lodgings. What rejoicings there must have been. The monks sang their thanks so loudly that even the early summer wind could not carry the sounds away. The soldiers had to put up with it and count the days.

Few things help to embellish a legend like the passing of eight hundred years. And there is more than one tale told about how the Cathedral came to be built by the river at Salisbury.

So glad were the Norman soldiers to see the backs of the monks at Old Sarum that, according to one story, they provided their strongest bowman, bending his most pliable bow, and firing his swiftest arrow into the distance from the hilltop fort. Where the arrow fell, there the new Cathedral would be built. At that distance, however, the story would have had to stretch more than the bow. To give it more logic another account says that the arrow struck a deer who galloped to the bank of the Avon before dropping dead. In another version the deer becomes a cow.

Centuries later a poet, Walter Pope, wrote his "Salisbury Ballad" in which the soldier tells the bishop that he has fired his bow:

"As far as that cow in Merry-field
Which grazes under the thorn."
The bishop asks "Where is Merry-field?"
And the soldier replies "By the riverside.
"Where you see that Brindle cow."

It seems odd that the bishop did not know Merry-field because he owned it. Perhaps he did not recognise its nickname. He knew it as Mary-field and the Cathedral today is dedicated to St. Mary the Virgin.

There are variant versions of the tale, one of which suggests that the monks of Old Sarum were thrown off their hill because of spending nights of excitement with nuns at the convenient convent at Wilton. It would be interesting to know how they got back. The vision of bleary friars, three to a mule perhaps, turning up at daylight at the portcullis and asking to be let in is an enticing one.

Whatever the truth, Merry-field, Myrie-field, or Mary's Field, was the chosen place for the new Cathedral. It was close on a hundred acres of fine grass, running down to a poetic river bank. What today would be called a choice piece of real estate.

A cathedral is not built in a day. Some have taken a thousand years, some are never finished. Salisbury took 38 years and was assembled by 300 men. The meadows were boggy but, miraculously, there was one strong area where the ground was pure gravel. They began delving there and they needed to go down less than *six feet.* The 2,500 tons of the spire, added over the next fifty-seven years, was almost confidently supported by the same depth of grit. Almost, because it has slipped two feet six inches and the interior columns are visibly bent. When we lived in The Walton Canonry we used to calculate that it would not miss us by much; the roof of our present house, just outside the Harnham Gate to the Cathedral Close is about the same distance. The spire remains resolute.

Walk to the West Front of the Cathedral today and look up at its sculptured gallery of figures, posed and poised. The niches are occupied by famously holy men who sometimes crumble leaving their space like an empty shelf in a shop. But Bishop Poore stands proud, clutching a model of his marvellous invention – which rises high before your eyes.

Go into the shadows of the building and you will find another man, a different man, his likeness only put there, apparently as an afterthought, sixty years ago – Elias Dereham – a workaholic genius. In 1946 he was remembered aptly by the local Freemasons because, although there were many others labouring on the building, eyeing it, pursing their lips, measuring with their fingers and thumbs, it was the stoneworkers, the masons, who saw it rise at the very tips of their noses.

Rough and ready gangs of masons used to roam England in those times, looking for work. They travelled with their carts and horses and even oxen and generally they did not have to seek long. The Normans built 170 new towns after the Conquest. The Romans had opted for artistic ingenuity, the Normans raw skill and muscle. And there was plenty of demand – not the least of it in Salisbury. The town was growing as the Cathedral grew and as The Close, with its clerical houses grew. They had jobs for life.

Wherever they settled, guarding their trade secrets and their tools, they made a camp, built shelters, and, when they missed them, sent for their wives and children. These shanty-towns were called lodges – a definition retained today by the Freemasons in many a suburb.

They were often hard and difficult men, drinking in the town's new taverns almost as soon as they had put the roofs in place. They also knew their commercial worth. Elias de Dereham must have had every shred of his Christian patience tried at times. Going on strike was obligatory. The Cathedral builders downed chisels and walked out over a pay claim for a penny-farthing a day. They returned to their lodges, sulked and would not shift until they won it. The place, today, is called Pennyfarthing Street. It is the address of the Salisbury District Council office where they currently collect our Council Tax, significantly more than a penny-farthing.

Today's stonemasons remain with a never-ending task. There are nine of them plus an apprentice. Their dusty yard is next to the Cathedral wall, as close to their work as they can be, although the Dean and Chapter would like them to move to a nice well-ordered trading estate, and keep nudging them in that direction so that more of the Close could be given to visitors. As ever the masons are stubborn, they do not want to go.

When we lived at The Walton Canonry there abruptly arose over the peaceful vista of Salisbury Cathedral and its delicate Close an unbelievably grandiose plan to turn it all into an enhanced money-magnet with new roads, coach parks, and a flyover or a fly-by of the River Avon. There was a horrifying scheme to eventually apron the Cathedral with a huge cobbled courtyard "like a continental cathedral".

Five thousand pairs of hands were thrown up in horror although the Dean and Chapter appeared to believe it was not at all a bad idea. The Times worriedly reported it. The stonemasons would be herded off to their cosy trading estate, their yard turned into a place for foreign charabancs.

We were invited to dinner at a grand home in what is, in more ways than one, upper Wiltshire. It was a storm-tossed night and the main door suddenly flew open and deposited Prince Charles almost into the lap of my wife. As we were processing towards the table, the Prince said to Hugh Dickinson, the amiable Dean: "What's this I hear from Salisbury?" Nervously the Dean told him of the widespread scheme and His Royal Highness sniffed: "I should bloody well forget that."

In the Close there were protests, campaigns and, considering the overall gentility of the attendance, some distinctly raucous meetings. At each of these, sitting at the back, was a silent, almost ghostly representative of the stonemasons. The grand plan was eventually dropped and everybody went home.

⌒⅊⌒

Alongside the high and mighty splendour of the Cathedral the yard of the stonemasons is a rough and dusty place, three sheds, and some piles of old stones. They have always had a cat mooching about the gritty corners and one, Ginger, has become immortalised in glass.

In the 1970's a stained glass window was unveiled depicting the laying of the five foundation stones seven hundred years before. Bishop Poore is there, of course, and Elias de Dereham, and Nicholas of Ely, the master mason, also Lord Salisbury (the first nobleman to be buried in the nave, who may well have been murdered). And Ginger the cat. He sits as cats do, comfortably, despite being a gross anachronism, watching the proceedings with all the attention of the ancient cloaked and crowned participants. They have a cat in the stonemasons' yard today. They share him with the elaborate surroundings next door.

Cats like cathedrals; there is ample territory, places to sleep (like the Bishop's Throne), shade in the summer and warm corners in the winter. They also know where the mice live.

My neighbours, Stephen and Kate Abbott, brought their own cat when they came to live in The Close. Both are teachers and Stephen is a lay vicar. Their cat was called Simpkin after the one in Beatrix Potter's 'The Tailor of Gloucester'. When they moved into their house by the Harnham Gate, Simpkin promptly deserted and went back to their former house on the other side of Salisbury, strolling over busy roads. She learned her lesson and when she was returned she stayed put, never to stray again. She was familiar with every ancient niche in the Cathedral and liked to taunt Taffy, the organist's dog. One Palm Sunday she joined in the procession following behind the donkey carrying Jesus.

In the stonemasons' dusty enclosure you can see the same tools and implements that were used when the first walls went up and are still used today – the pitcher and punch, the claw chisel, the mallet with a heft of apple wood.

Today's master mason is impressed with the work of his long-gone predecessors. "Some of the stones we replace now have been there since the beginning," he says. He points to a drawing on a plinth. "And they did not even have pencils and paper."

Despite its pale face, Chilmark stone is hefty stuff but the masons daily chivvy and chamfer to produce delicate faces for replacement angels and gargoyles, crooked grins, happy smiles, and knowing looks. But in the workshop not every bit of history is ancient. Half-hidden by the door was a life sized figure with a Second World War steel helmet covering its forehead, a pair of goggles on its face and a gasmask. I did not like to ask who it was.

CHAPTER 3

Inspired Builders

TODAY, IF YOU CLIMB SIXTY feet up into the tower of the Cathedral you will come across a human-sized treadmill. If anyone has wondered, and many have, how the tons of stone were hoisted to the upper walls then here is the answer. It is an ancient reproduction of the wooden machines which did the job even earlier. Two men (or four depending on the load) inserted themselves into the drum of the mill where they could stand and wedge themselves. Then, like large mice, they would tread in unison, doubtless humming some popular song of the day. How long their turn was I have not found recorded but when they were tired another team would take their places. And so the stones, carved and curved, the baulks of timber and all the other materials were lifted to the ever-rising workface.

When later generations came to build the spire, they

worked from the inside as if constructing a tunnel into the sky and then crawled up through it to build some more. Much of the scaffolding, wood and metal was left in place, and some of it remains up there today, the early fragments lost in age and cobwebs.

Lead for the roof was boiled, shaped and cooled in the plumbery which is now the refectory, where you can get the most astonishing view of the spire up through the glass ceiling, and a Sunday roast, good value at ten pounds ninety-five.

In the year 1220 they began hauling the blocks of lard-coloured Chilmark stone from a quarry twelve miles to the west. It is still cut there today; the quarrymen will point to the holes from whence Salisbury Cathedral was chopped out. Twelve miles sounds conveniently near but the road was a matter of conjecture, impassable in the winter months, and a trying journey for the rest of the year.

The King gave timber from his oaks at Alderbury, on the edge of the neighbouring New Forest. Again, it does not seem a far journey but it is loose, wet and stony under hoof.

Alice Bruer, a noblewoman from Dorset, donated twelve years' supply of Purbeck stone and marble. You can see the coloured marble today, suspiciously bowed and bent where the roof has fidgeted.

Even by car it is not a straightforward journey from the Purbeck quarries but my thought is that Lady Alice reached back even further into history to solve it. One of the more plausible answers to the mystery of how the gigantic stones were brought from Wales to Stonehenge before anyone could write a witness account, is that they came by sea. They were loaded onto rafts or barges on the Welsh coast and voyaged down the Bristol Channel and around the edge of Cornwall until, after a strenuous and dangerous trip, they arrived at the mouth of the River Avon at Christchurch. Then they were floated up the sturdy stream to a point near Salisbury and then ox-and-man handled the last twenty miles or so.

I believe, and there are those who will argue, that Lady Bruer adopted the same method. She had the marble slabs transported along the coast and then sailed them up-river. Less than two miles downstream from Salisbury is St. Peter's ancient church at Britford, with the Avon running almost past its porch. Against the north wall of the chancel is a tomb incorporating a hefty slab of Purbeck marble. It is said to be the grave of the Duke of Buckingham, executed in what is now Debenham's Store, Salisbury, in 1483, but it is made up of various stone oddments and, in fact, may not even be the unfortunate Duke's tomb. There are various possibilities – on the other hand there may be nobody at home at all. The tomb may be empty. The church has some other oddities. There is an entry in the parish register: "Widow Tongue. 15 Jan. 1650 Nil nisi lingua" ('Nothing but tongue')

There is another piece of Purbeck marble on a window sill in the chancel. It has been fashioned into an effigy but was found embedded in a wall. Could it be that these blocks of Purbeck were bound up-river for the builders of Salisbury Cathedral? Could it be they fell from the back of a barge?

≈

In the days when he was a reluctant schoolmaster, needless to say before he became a Nobel Prizewinner, William Golding could look from his classroom window and see the magnificent serenity of Salisbury Cathedral Spire – aptly framed.

Apart from 'Lord of the Flies' he wrote a novel called 'The Spire' but ever denied he had taken inspiration from that view, a denial even less convincing than Trollope's rebuttal of tales that his Barchester novels were based on Salisbury characters. Added to this, Golding always said that the boys of the English class at Bishop Wordsworth's Grammar School, within The Close, bore no relation to those strange and disturbing characters portrayed in 'Lord of the Flies'. The only way he used his captive pupils, apparently, was to scan the pages of his scribbled manuscript for obvious errors and, importantly in those days before laptops, count the number of words.

With four hundred and four feet of slender uncertainty hanging above him, as he faced the boys droning their way through afternoon verbs, the description of the collapse of such a structure in 'The Spire' must have literally fallen onto the page. There was the terrible fear among the worshippers that the great four columns of Golding's fictional spire would "open apart like a flower and . . . stone, wood, iron, glass, men would slide down into the church . . ." But no, he insisted, the book had no connection with Salisbury.

But churches, even cathedrals, used to fall down quite readily in the early days. The builders had to make it up as they climbed and they were open to miscalculation. In France, Tours Cathedral fell down *twice*.

St Edmund's, one of Salisbury's oldest churches, only a stroll through the streets from the Cathedral, spectacularly fell down, or at least its tower did. The churchwardens had grown concerned that the ringing of the bell in 1651 was doing no good to the belfry and they stopped tolling it. Two years later, during a full service attended by the mayor and 'a great multitude of Godly Christians', according to the church records, "The maine pillars did bulge out and sensibley shake. The clefts in the walls were seen to open and shut." And that was at the ringing of the single Sermon Bell; that day it must have been a shortish sermon.

"Nothing but the Will of God did keep the stones and timber from falling . . ." reported the churchwardens.

On the Monday morning they <u>did</u> fall – when the church was empty. A miracle!

No man ever so much as suggested that the fragile Salisbury Cathedral should be trusted with heavyweight bells. Today, the call to worship at this grand building is sounded by one verger pulling one rope tolling one bell. Some people have brought along their own bells. I have seen a wedding party engulfed by dinging and donging, coming from C.D. players at full volume. Unofficial, of course. The Cathedral bell has a lonely but not unlovely call. In summer it sounds for the earliest communion when the birds are just awake and the river is shining; in winter it signals the cosy chanting of evensong as the afternoon fades outside the windows.

It was a daring feat to attempt to build the spire at all. No one had ever put up a soaring structure like that, not since Babel anyway, and Richard of Farleigh, the latest in a line of visionary master-masons, must have had doubts every day.

His men were climbing into the sky over Salisbury, literally feeling their way through thin air, making it up as they went. At its base the cone is two feet thick, tapering to nine inches at the cross-crowned summit. It took less than half-a-century to build and the intrepid men clung on in all weathers, finishing undoubtedly with a great sense of attainment not to mention relief.

The first threat to the steeple, and the Cathedral below it, came from a strange source – doves. The cooing invaders, in their thousands, had colonised the spire and much of the nave and cloisters. The clerks, the clergy and the choir, set about getting rid of the nests filling the dim rising void. There was smoke and bows and arrows, and a lot of feathers before the menace was eventually defeated. These days birds stay mainly outside.

At one time it was a sport for local boys (and the more agile of the choristers) to climb to the top of the spire, finishing the adventure by clinging to the hooped metal staples that occasional steeplejacks still hang onto today.

There is a tale of a Salisbury clockmaker who wound his watch while leaning on the uppermost pediment; another concerns a boy supposedly standing on his head at the same place. Why either did it has never been explained. The plumber called Halley carried his leg of mutton and "two fowles" up there and enjoyed a hearty meal. Once again, why he needed to do this has never been fully told. If asked at the time of their feat, each of these spire-climbers would probably have replied, using something of the mountaineer's traditional answer: "Because it is there."

The spire is given a studied wide berth by overflying

ducks, geese, swans and light aircraft. Generations of peregrine falcons have visited and left the remnants of their dinners for naturalists and sweepers-up. The falcon obviously enjoys the lofty privacy of cathedrals. At Chichester this year, one has laid three eggs on a dizzy ledge.

There is a special serenity to be found up there. Exhibitionists no longer scale the spire and there is little more to be found than sun and rain and wind. Sacred relics which were placed when the first builders had reached the top they had just made, are still mainly undisturbed, although the cross surmounting everything has not been allowed a quiet life. When it was brought down for a rare inspection it was found to be drilled by several bullet holes. Since it's almost unthinkable that some loitering peace-time pilot would have fired a few bursts out of boredom, they appear to date from the air battles of World War Two. Ours or theirs?

Anything projecting four hundred and more feet into the clouds is bound to have an attraction for random forks of lightning. The spire has been a sitting target. In May, 1560, Bishop Jewel recorded that it had not only been struck but had been so "shattered by lightning that a continued fissure was made from the top for sixty feet downwards." In June, 1741, after another storm, smoke was seen seeping, then pouring from the tower. All the townspeople turned out to rescue their treasured landmark and, with brave bucket-chains, managed to douse the fire in two hours. Another hour and there would have been nothing for later visitors to view, except debris. You can today still see the scorch marks within the tower.

But it was a plumber (not our friend Halley) who put the whole edifice in grave danger. His carelessness caused an outbreak of fire which was only extinguished by, once again, the efforts of the neighbours. The accounts of the Cathedral Clerk of Works make it sound thirsty work: *"A Byle for charges at the Fyer making yow Pay Noe More than I pay to the Brewer . . .*

"A Hamerkin of Strong Beer	*12 shillings and 9 pence*
Three barrels of Small Beer	*10 shillings and 1 and a half pence*
For some people that would drinke Brandy one pint cost	*6 pence*
Some people that stayed about to see the Fyer out after all the rest were gon being people that looks for nothing for their Paynes	*2 shillings*
For Pipes and Bread and Cheese	*1 shilling*
Total:	*£1.6.4 and a half pence.*

They had the Drinke and tapt theirselves, and drew it out, I look not for a Peny Profit."

That seems to adequately paint the picture. Even those who look for nothing for their paynes cost two shillings. It seems to have been a jolly night. How did they contrive to put the fire out?

There was one further expense. A widow called Lane of "St. Marting parish" asked for help from the Dean so that she might be kept from perishing. She had caught a violent sickness carrying buckets of water to fight the fire that night. She was saved by half-a-crown.

Risks are even greater these days, despite a lightning conductor keeping the topmost cross company. Regularly everyone is cleared from the Cathedral, even the press being excluded, while the Wiltshire Fire Brigade sends its men climbing and clambering at speed through corners and niches of the building no one else ever sees. The huge burnished fire engines arrive with their mechanical ladders and their cherry pickers, although how they get them through the crevice of the main arch is a mystery. There can scarcely be half an inch clearance each side and they come through like a bolt of lightning, although maybe that is not apt. From the Salisbury fire station to the Cathedral West Door takes no more than three minutes.

For the emergency men, anywhere in The Close is top priority and, even before we had moved into The Walton Canonry we had evidence of this. One evening a retired surgeon, Philip Shemilt, who recently died after living in The Close for half a century, saved our house from burning down. He was practising his golf shots on the cricket ground when he saw a finger of smoke curling from an upstairs window. Dropping his nine iron he ran the two hundred yards to Sir Edward Heath's house and shouted to the security guards. It only took minutes for the firemen to arrive and deal with the smoulder. Another ten and the entire beautiful house, with its ancient wooden roof and windows would have been an uncontrollable bonfire.

Not unlike the Cathedral's careless plumber a few centuries before, a workman with a blowtorch had overlooked some smouldering sawdust. Our builder mentioned that only that day he had insured the building for a million pounds.

⚶

Outside the bulwark of the Cathedral Wall, across Exeter Street, at one time called Dragon Street, is a first floor window framing a vision of the Spire which until recently rivalled the view which William Golding had from his English Class just across the street.

Mr. and Mrs. John Faulkner, my son-in-law and my daughter, who live in Spire House, take their Bed & Breakfast guests to the front room to view the spire against the sky. It used to be a better scene but Bishop Wordsworth's Grammar School has built an extension which cuts the lower half out. They still have most of the spire to see and the occasional drama. Routine maintenance at 404 feet above the ground is always absorbing, even from a distance. Men climb up the outside of the slope, perhaps to service the red warning light that tells aircraft and swans to keep their distance. The ascending men are securely fastened but it is still a long way to climb to change a light bulb and a helicopter always hangs about nearby.

For a week in the slow season Diana and I took over the Spire House Bed & Breakfast so that the owners could take a break. (It deserves a book to itself: One very elderly lady with an elderly husband, wedged in among their many belongings in an elderly car, drove – one stop – from Blackpool and having been disinterred from her luggage asked if we could put her supply of jam sandwiches in the fridge.

Our pleasure was at night with the Cathedral Spire rising across the street, like a silent watchman looking over the sleeping roofs of the city.

There is a marvellous 50 year old photograph of two steeplejacks perched casually on some spidery scaffolding and in the early nineteen fifties a lead cup was found lodged on the capstone. It contained a relic of The Virgin Mary and was carried down for keeping in the Cathedral Archives.

During our time in The Walton Canonry we often saw miniature men clinging to the spire. There was a real risk of it tumbling down then together with large lumps of the Cathedral and millions were raised to keep it more or less upright. Prince Charles and Princess Diana sat through a concert in aid of the cause on a summer evening that was uniquely cold and became colder. Blankets were brought for the royal legs. But their personal atmosphere was just as frosty. It was one of their last evenings together

One day there was a mishap high on the steeple. We could see men crawling about their platform of poles. A helicopter chugged over The Close and edged by the inch towards the lofty place. It hung with amazing cleverness within touching distance of the skin of the spire. The man was handed across. People in The Close and in the Salisbury streets, who had watched transfixed, started to clap but I don't imagine they were heard up there. It was all on the television news that night.

⁓

On a drab day the Cathedral looks drab. Its stones take on a workaday solidity, its windows scarcely blink and the spire is only a spire, high but not much on a photograph. Even Constable found it necessary to cheat, to add a touch of pink to the colour of the masonry.

But it only needs a sliver of sun, a curtain of cloud pulled away, a subtle alteration in the light, and it can become celestial. And moonlight becomes it. On a bright night it is touched with wonder.

One winter's evening, returning home on foot, we let ourselves in through one of the great gates (residents' keys) and stepped into a world of deep frost and silence. There was a crackling in the air, white underfoot, trees standing speechless. We were the only people there; we might easily have been the only people in the world. As we stepped, so oddly careful, our steps sounded sharp, concise as gunshots.

The floodlights of the Cathedral are half-buried in the ground among the old submerged graves, and as they shone, slanting up the walls and buttresses, they threw a ghostly shadow of the spire into the dark sky, the cross at the summit supporting its own image as if it were standing on its own head.

We walked home without speaking. We knew we lived in a special place.

CHAPTER 4

The Disappearing Wren

IT SEEMS ASTONISHING THAT OF all the clever, noble and notable men connected with Salisbury, the genius Sir Christopher Wren is the one who has left the least trace.

Wren surveyed the Cathedral at the behest of his friend, Bishop Seth Ward, one of a colourful procession of bishops and a founder of The Royal Society, the brilliant brains of the arts and scientists, of which Wren was a member. The Bishop did not like the way in which the spire appeared to be leaning. Wren confirmed his suspicions. It was two feet six inches out of true. But attempts to credit Wren with anything beyond a couple of minor carved panels and some advice on the choir stalls, have failed. His poetic notebooks, written and drawn with delicacy and by his own hand, are still in the Cathedral archives as poignant and practical memories but most other evidence, if there ever was any, has vanished with the years.

Knowing fingers have been pointed towards the fine Matrons' College, almshouses for the widows of the clergy, with its Wren-like touches, which capture the eye and attention as you enter the North Gate of the Close. The College was founded by Bishop Ward (rumour having it that he wanted to give a home to a poor clergy widow who had turned down his marriage proposal many years before. Even a bishop can be in love. No one ever found out which of the ten widows living there was the stubborn one). Who drew the plans for the pleasing terrace with its vivid Royal Coat of Arms of Charles the Second is not known, although the cost was £1,193. The building work was that of Thomas Glover of Harnham, just around the corner, who is credited on his tombstone with "stately, curious and artful edifices". Could it be this local builder worked under the eye of Christopher Wren?

Apart from his elegant notebooks in the Archives the only sure evidence of Wren's hand is his survey of 1669 which brought him to the conclusion that the spire was out of kilter. His calculations stand to this day and are marked by a plumb line which drops to a brass plaque set in the floor at the centre of the tower. It has not wavered an inch since. The plumb line is examined by flocks of slightly dubious tourists (who invariably then turn squeezed eyes up to the void within the spire above). Nobody has contradicted him yet.

Wren's epitaph in St. Paul's Cathedral is the famous advice to those who looking for it – translated from the Latin – "Reader, if you seek his monument - look about you". In Salisbury his reputation hangs by a thread.

There is a ladies' fashion shop a few steps beyond the main arched gate to The Close and the Cathedral and from there, on occasions, a figure emerges arrayed in more colour and splendour than any of the female clientele would attempt. It is the Bishop of Salisbury.

The shop is among the city's oldest buildings, (some say its first). It is called Mitre House and it was here that Bishop Poore lodged while his Cathedral was being built eight centuries ago. When a new Bishop is enthroned he still changes into his elaborate raiment there in a room reserved for that purpose. It is one of the ways that Salisbury tends not merely to protect its past but to adapt it and use it.

The finest house built for the most outstanding and outrageous of its citizens in the 16th century still has its everyday use. John Hall's Hall, with its cavern of a lobby making for a fine foyer, now houses the Odeon Cinema with its multi-screens and its preservation status. Hall was a rich and sometimes violent man; he cursed before royalty and behaved as he pleased. He had a ship harboured at Poole, twenty-five miles away, which occasionally indulged in a little privateering (until it unknowingly stole a cargo belonging to the king).

Some of Hall's adventures have only been bettered by the Hollywood productions shown on the screens in what was his grand home. It became the country's only cinema with a listed status when it opened in 1931 as the Gaumont British Wonder Theatre. The main feature was "A Yankee in King Arthur's Court" which John Hall might well have enjoyed.

Even the site of the execution of The Duke of Buckingham is still in busy everyday use. It is now Debenham's store. The Duke's headless ghost is sometimes appropriately seen in the millinery department.

⁓⁓⁓

Unlike most cities where the cathedral was tacked onto an existing place, the streets of Salisbury rose around the rising spire and the arranged houses of The Close. They were set out like Manhattan centuries later, on a grid system, a pattern of aptly named chequers.

Each chequer was a self-contained plot, enough for a house or a small tenement, a scrap of land perhaps, or a business, or a pub. There were more than twenty, mostly to the north and north west of the city, and each had a name, many of which remain today, although scarcely a stone stands of what once was there.

There was The Three Cups Chequer, Mr. Rolphe's Chequer, and Mr. Mundeye's Blue Boar, Cross Keys and the Three Swans in Rollestone Street, the nearest guess suggesting that it was the route for blocks of masonry to be rolled towards the building site of the Cathedral, although there once was a Canon Rollestone living in The Close. Gigant Street, which is adjoining, may be a later misspelling of Giant Street where the Salisbury Giant, a startling twelve foot ogre rather oddly riding a hobby horse, was paraded on celebration days. He now scowls, but frightens no-one, in the Museum in The Close.

What was novel about the streets was that many of them

had watercourses, narrow canals, running downhill through them. At first these channels (New Canal Street which is still busy but without running water, is one that is remembered) progressed down the centre of the road but, as it eventually occurred to the inhabitants, so did the many horses. The canals provided a handy receptacle for waste. They became little more than open sewers, everyone threw anything in them, and eventually along came cholera.

Some tried to conceal the problem by calling Salisbury "the English Venice" but it never washed. The town could be smelled even further away than the spire could be seen. The main waterway, which sludged by the market with its slaughtering butchers and fishmongers, was uncompromisingly called The Town Ditch. Everything went into The Town Ditch, including, after a spring-clean at the Cathedral, a priceless stained glass window. Years later, a modern cleric, the Rev. Stanley Baker, even tried to trace its whereabouts, delving and digging and following ancient documents. What is more, he partially succeeded, but nobody wanted the fine window, or what remained of it. Some of it had even been used as hardcore during road-building!

So many of the early street names still hang out at corners that it is possible to pick your way around the houses by using John Speed's map of 1611. Some names have been changed of course, not entirely for the better, and Salisbury has, within the last fifty years built the ultimately useless road – the road to nowhere. It was part of a planning scheme, a pattern of unsuitably whirling highways that would take traffic high above the rooftops. And that is where it stayed, hanging above the rooftops, but with no definable destination and no traffic. It was a pity there was already a highway in the city called Endless Street.

⌒ℳ⌒

One of the less noble and less notable legends of the Age of Chivalry was that of the knight who stole a communion wafer from Salisbury Cathedral and smuggled it home to eat with an onion for his supper. It must have been a big wafer or a small onion. As a penance for his gluttony the knight is said to have financed the Market Cross at the corner of the market square, still very evident today where the one-way system passes Toni & Guy (smart hairdressers), Boots the Chemist, Dr. China (Chinese herbal remedies), Starbucks, Holland & Barrett, etc. Even at 14th century prices it must have been cheaper for him to buy a late-night take away.

The cross has been rebuilt and given a scrub every few years but there it remains like a stony crown for a large king. The market vendors once sold chickens and ducks there, and at Christmas the odd goose; and country people with their fruit and vegetables were spread around its steps.

Not much changed during the centuries. The market is still held on Tuesdays and Saturdays as it has been since established by Royal Decree in 1227. It was the masterstroke in the establishment of the city. With the Cathedral, rising confidently in the background, it brought trade and people and wealth.

The rowdy cattle have now been shifted to a site on the edge of town. Chopper-heaving men in Butchers' Row used to slaughter them to order on the pavement. An ox standing eighteen hands and weighing 120 stones once appeared in the market but its fate is unrecorded.

Chipper Lane was where the chippers, the sharp-talking chapmen, the street traders, plied and lied. There was Fish Row, Ox Row, Salt Lane, Oatmeal Row, Mealmonger Street (also called Milkmonger Street) and Cordwainer Street. In the courtyards and alleys all around, it was bedlam. Two thousand sheep, straight from the fresh air of Salisbury Plain, were herded into the noisy confines on some days. There was avid drinking in the market-side pubs, peep-shows, quack doctors and quacking ducks, and you could throw rotten cabbage at the malefactors in the town stocks or chorus the lashes doled out at the whipping post. A good time was had by nearly all.

Look at the rooftops around the market square now and you see the same slopes and outlines as shown by Rowlinson and other long-gone artists. Today the trade is still in vegetables and meat (we get our organic chicken sausages there), in knicker elastic and second-hand books. People come from miles to see and buy just as they always did.

Three times a year there is a fair, in August, in October, at Michaelmas and a Lady Day Fair during Lent. They originated with the market and most of the profits were taken by the Bishop who also did well from the market. Once they had wrestling and spangled acrobats, now it's dodgem cars and bingo. Everybody who can walk in Salisbury goes to the fair. One of the former pupils of William Golding at Bishop Wordsworth's School recalls seeing the Nobel Prize author there with his beard lost in a mass of candyfloss. It is that sort of occasion.

Thirty years ago, during our adventurous and nomadic marriage, for some reason we had a small-holding, about five miles from Salisbury, with pigs and cows, some chickens and lots of foxes. On the hill was a stone-age signal place, from where a warning fire could be seen from a far-off look-out in the next county. Being amateur farmers we were, of course, reluctant to send any of our animals to market (en route for a slaughterhouse) but one morning Diana took a heifer (for 'growing on') to Salisbury cattle market. The mean men around the auction ring had dark faces, squashed caps and old coats tied with string. They bawled at the terrified animals and beat them with thick walking sticks. Diana was not having any of this institutional cruelty and, slight and scared, she marched into the ring with her heifer, and defied the Hogarthian rabble. There was ribaldry and the rudest of comments, but she stuck with her cow.

It was an heroic act. What knight with his wafer and onion could compare?

CHAPTER 5

Who Stole the Wall?

IT HAS BEEN A MYSTERY for centuries, but rarely mentioned because it is one of those mysteries to which most people guess the answer. What happened to approximately four hundred massive yards of The Close and Cathedral Wall? If it were stolen (purloined would be more polite) how was it done? Why was an ecclesiastical blind eye turned in the direction of a mass theft?

The castellated walls on three sides of The Close – with a few minor inroads – have stood sturdily at 13 feet tall and unmovably broad since they were built to defend and enhance the situation of the new Cathedral. But a defence is hardly effective if one side is gone widely missing. The Western flank was built alongside the river, thus doubly strengthened. It ran, so the guesswork suggests, from west of the main gate to the bank of the Avon and then curved south to beyond what is today the house of the Bishop, The South Canonry. It was a big wall. But the only sign of it now is a stump of stone in the garden of The North Canonry, which in our time was the home of a remarkable woman, Mrs. Olga Cory. She called it "our solitary tooth" and that is how it looks.

Otherwise, along the entire supposed length of this heavy fortification, there is scarcely a single lump of masonry, no sign of a footing, hardly a clue that it was there. It once ran behind the houses of the West Walk, including ours, and yet you would never have known it. On the other hand our house, built in 1720 of elegant Georgian brick, was shored up at basement level with blocks of strange stone.

The finger of suspicion points unwaveringly in the direction of the Canons themselves. In the eighteenth century they were building the second generation of Close houses along the river and there is little doubt that, bit by bit, they helped themselves to the wall. Even an augustly official publication such as The Royal Commission on the Historical Monuments of England cannot escape the carefully worded conclusion ". . . no doubt there is a general connection between the appearance of architectural stonework along the West side of The Close and the disappearance of the wall".

Not that by the early eighteenth century an invasion by raiding Goths was anticipated. The wall had become an adornment, apparently a disposable one.

From my view, as I write, I look down on the face of the

wall – one of its many faces – standing grey and strong like a sturdy old man. Behind it, from this window, are the trees of autumn vivid with colour, bright reds, deep auburns, different greens. It is their last performance of the year. Winter is coming. That the wall was built to demonstrate the prestige of the Cathedral and its skirt of The Close is beyond doubt. How much it was counted upon as a defence is more arguable.

Almost from the setting of the foundations of the town there had grown a rivalry amounting to animosity between the Salisbury citizens and the robed men of the church. Ownership, rates and taxes, personal dislikes and disdain developed into rank enmity. Bishop Ayscough was assassinated by a mob led by a Salisbury butcher. The question was – who was going to man the battlements of the Godly wall? Certainly no town militia as they were more likely to constitute the enemy. The clergy, many elderly, were unlikely to stand defiance; they were preachers not bow and pike men. The garrison, unless substantial platoons could have been marched from a distance, would have been thin on the ramparts.

The assault never took place, although the sounds coming from the crammed city streets continued to be disgruntled for many years. The town's big-mouthed leaders, as epitomised by the brash and boastful John Hall, poured mud into the entrance to The Close and scorn on the people inside. Hall himself was once thrown into the local prison (which he owned) for his excesses. Once the Dean of Salisbury stood outside the Cathedral's West Door and dared the Mayor of the town to just *try* and bring the civic mace into the sacred nave. It was the nearest the church and the city ever came to open warfare.

When the walls of the new Cathedral were rising Elias de Dereham had a ditch dug around the ecclesiastical land. It proved useful not only as a deterrent to intruders but as a place to throw rubbish. The wall he began is still in one piece today, fitted alongside Salisbury's streets, looking with a grey impassive expression on local buses. It was constructed from stone rubble from the Cathedral building but many of the sturdy blocks were hauled by oxen and men from the former settlement of Old Sarum. By now the garrison soldiers had gone home, the hovels of the hilltop town had been deserted, and both the original Cathedral and the Norman castle were left to be rent by the noisy wind. Few people ever lived up there again. At the time of Old Sarum's nineteenth century notoriety as a "Rotten Borough", sending unelected men to Parliament there were exactly seven names on the voting list. But in these early times stone was precious. You can detect it today set into The Close wall, stone of a different hue, in some places oddly embossed with the face of a flower, a star, a spoked wheel or a sacred cross.

They transported it by the ton and the wall grew, thirteen feet high, club-footed, with battlements, look-out places, a walkway and lavatories ominously overlooking the town ditch. In later times hardy choirboys used to run novel obstacle races along the top, chanting Latin lamentations and limericks as they scrambled.

People who live in The Close now often find signs left for them by craftsmen who have long gone. A carpenter's initials incised in an ancient beam, a plumber's thumb print in a pipe, and if you replace a window pane you often find a message from some seventeenth century glazier.

The house next to ours during our ten years, Myles Place, had most of its Georgian windows reduced to shards by the explosion of a super-banger rocket in its front garden during a firework display. Salisbury, for all its historic fragility, was always keen on pyrotechnics; making fireworks is a local industry. Hundreds pounds worth of windows had to be repaired at Myles Place and a whole register of old glaziers was revealed. When we needed to replace a pane we always carefully scraped away the crumbly putty and uncovered the evidence: "A.J. Sals. 1784". But they left no further messages.

Stonemasons also delighted in leaving their trademarks, although it must have taken them longer. No fewer than a hundred and thirty marks are still to be seen on the otherwise impassive masonry of The Close wall. They look like some secret agent's cipher or a riddle from a tomb in ancient Egypt. Only other stonemasons would know who had cut them. There is a swastika, the traditional sign for good fortune, a few recognisable letters from our alphabet, some of them carved at angles as if the craftsman was working in an awkward position; what could a bull with big horns or a pair of largish bosoms mean? There are arrows and crosses and what looks sombrely like a coffin. Not one has ever been deciphered.

There were strongpoints on the wall through which arrows could be fired and places convenient for pitching boiling pitch on the heads of enemies. When the threat of battles faded, however, windows began to appear and doors into the houses within. There were always four gates, the main North Gate, the St. Ann's Gate (the 'Tann Gate', as the townspeople called it; either an abbreviation of 'St. Ann' or a twisting of "town") and the Harnham Gate which is almost outside my present study window. The Palace Gate was the Bishop's private entry. From the very start they were always shut at night, with a great clang of finality by the watchman. By eleven you cannot get in or out unless you have a key.

During Oliver Cromwell's time there was a gate knocked through the wall to give access to the Bishop's Palace which, at that puritan period, was used as a hostelry doing bed and breakfast.

Each of the gates hid its own secrets and its own story. The builders who fashioned them left even more explicit reminders of who they were. There is a pathetic sense of men seeking personal immortality, or at least publicity. Within the Palace Gate, now the entrance to the Cathedral School, is elaborately carved "M. Brown. 1708" and "I. H. 1751". A 16th century worker called "Galeyon" cut his name on the doorway of the small chapel at the St. Ann Gate and a man who had nothing better to do at the time carved: "G. A. Act. 22 1699" nearby. Replaced glass from the Cathedral itself was transported for use in the main North Gate and this was etched with initials and dates from the 17th century.

The gates are still as accommodating as a house, all having several rooms including a jail at the main gate. It seems it was not infrequently occupied. There was often trouble in the town and a portcullis was pulled down on 15th Century nights. But, sometimes, the bothermakers came from within the Close itself.

A Vicar returning to his house within the wall one night had a fight with the gate-keeper who refused his entry because it was past the then curfew time of nine o'clock. The holy man punched the guard in the face and "grievously wounded" him. Another Vicar, a knight in his own right, Sir Richard Roebucke, struggled with an elderly gate-keeper Rober Dyer and called him an "old rattling churl" before striking him on the chest. Dyer was hurt by the insult more than the blow and wrote it down in evidence to be presented to the Dean – "OOlde rattlyng cherle". The grave insult can still be read today.

Rather than provoke trouble some of the gate guards would look away when a shadow of a hooded woman flitted past and headed for the door of one of the resident vicars. A man in the town complained that his wife spent all night in The Close at the house of a vicar, Thomas de Colne. The woman confessed to being at the vicar's call at any time. The Cathedral authorities threw de Colne out of the town and told him not to return. The lady was whipped through The Close.

The gatehouses would be recognisable today to the Salisbury of several hundred years ago. The primary North Gate has stood sturdily through history. Cromwell's reforms resulted in it being sold to a London Haberdasher, Alexander Hatchett, presumably as a holiday home, but at the Restoration of the Monarchy it was back in church ownership. Today, the coloured coat of arms of The Stuarts crowns the arch and for centuries the statue of one of the Stuart kings looked into The Close from the other side. There was eventually some doubt as to which king it depicted because rain had reduced it to little more than a stone pillar before he was taken down and replaced economically with bits and pieces of other monarchs. It ended up as a recognisable Edward the Seventh and he is still there.

During our time living there a surge of excitement went through the residents of what is, in effect, a small village. A lorry loaded with wine had become jammed under the arch of the main gate. It was transporting the wine from France to Ireland and the French driver had become confused and found himself off the main route and hopelessly creeping around the narrow corners of Salisbury. The more corners, the more confused he became. In the end he decided to make a dash for Milford Haven via the Cathedral Close. His vehicle wedged itself neatly and tightly below the historic North Gate. The royal coat of arms shuddered and the Close Constable's quarters shook. A lady working at a desk in the room overhead was frightened.

The truck was stuck. It took all of two days to de-wedge it. Eventually it was able to back out – taking some of the precious arch with it. Then, with its liquid cargo, it set off again for the distant Irish ferry. How any fire engine could have entered the vicinity of the Cathedral during those two days was doubtless accounted for.

In the beautiful room adjacent to the curved St. Ann's Gate, which is attached to Malmesbury House, George Frederic Handel played and composed his music. How much he did of either is not clear but he enjoyed his visits to his

friend, James Harris who, another contemporary, Dr.
Johnson, described as: "a prig and a bad prig." Prig or not,
Harris was a great patron of music and the arts, and his
concerts, some given at his house, were acclaimed both for
the musical guests and the hospitality. Handel was a large
German man with a large German humour and a copious
appetite. His local friend, the Earl of Radnor, once sent him
some prime burgundy at his house in Brook Street, London.
Handel had guests but abruptly sprang up exclaiming: "Ah
. . . I hav der taught!" People were used to these "thoughts",
these moments of inspiration, and fully understood when he
had to leave the room. He might be sliding off to write
another "Messiah". But once, one of the guests ill-
manneredly followed him and peered through the keyhole of
the room into which he had disappeared. He saw Handel
sitting, fat, private and happy, drinking Lord Radnor's
burgundy. He had no intention of sharing it. But he was
amiable and generous. Once, remembered Harris "I got him
to sit down at the harpsichord where he played for near half
an hour".

Another visitor to Malmesbury House was King Charles
the Second when he was a Prince. He stayed there during
troubled Cromwellian times in a small room, now beautifully
restored, and from a window spoke the soldiers guarding him
below in Exeter Street. The room had a cupboard which
concealed a narrow staircase to a room below with a door
leading to Exeter Street. Until quite recently there was also
access from the house to a tunnel below the street, now filled
in by the Council.

CHAPTER 6

The Rowdy Canons

APART FROM THE DUST CLOGGED organ abandoned in our cellar (which some guests in the room above, formerly a chapel, suggested they heard being ghostily played in dead of night) one other memento had been left to us when we moved into The Walton Canonry. It was a wooden panel upon which were the names of the previous occupants of the house going back to one, William of Cerdstock, in 1198. I never investigated the authenticity of this (and the family before us, as I have said, were not above jokes) but if it were genuine then William must have moved into The Close before anyone else; fifteen or more years before the other monks built their houses and moved in. Perhaps he lived in a tent.

It was not until 1213 that the decree was published that the canons should build "fair houses of stone" on plots of one and a half acres, with selected dwellings given larger areas – but all at their own expense. Some could not afford it. They each received an income from some outlying parish but sometimes this did not amount to much. Peter de Blois, scholar and secretary to the Bishop, protested that his prebend wage would not even cover his travelling expenses to Salisbury. He could not afford the fare.

Others had trouble raising the money and there was nothing to show on their building sites but weeds and wild flowers. By 1222 they were told to build or else. "Everyone who has a site must begin to build to some purpose by Whitsuntide, next ensuing, or failing this the bishop shall dispose of his site." The scaffolding began to go up.

What sort of men were these first householders in The Close? Some were holy, some barely stood up to inspection; some were mystic and some mountebanks. There was the blessed Brother Stephen who delighted in love and was "of so sweet a nature and of such joyousness . . . that he never allowed anyone so far as it was in his power, to be sad". A likeness to our jolly friend Canon Kerruish many centuries after him is tempting. When Brother Stephen died he, like John Kerruish, was sung into heaven by choristers. The only difference was that Brother Stephen himself, joyfully but probably croakily, led the chorus.

Then there was the priest who was a favourite of the king and his nobles because he gabbled through the prayers before hunting, thus enabling the hunters to mount and be quickly away to the chase.

Another holy householder, William Osgodby caused trouble by entertaining too long and too frequently Mistress Alicia Hoskyns, and there were others who stayed out late in the taverns.

Once some houses had been built, keeping pace with the rising of the new Cathedral, the canons enjoyed, between services and psalms, a warm and sometimes even unruly home life. A wintertime fire, central in the hall, with sparks and smoke flying up the chimney, was the place to pour wine and have a sing-song. Much of the singing was derived from the Latin praises sung during worship including a favourite known as the "Great Os". I have the music before me, for the magnificent Salisbury Choir still sing the antiphons to the Magnificat in the days up to Christmas. No one these days, even choristers, can explain it fully but this music had taken on the popularity of everyday song. It was always chorused around the fire with the wine and the fellowship and outsiders from the town itself often crowded the door to listen and even join in. Each part of the praise began with "O" which gave them their names: O Sepientia, O Adony, O Radix Jesse, and so on to O Rex Gentium, O Emmanuel and O Virgo Virginum. Somehow these holy portions had acquired nicknames, originating no doubt with the choirboys, so that one "pro le O" became "Le O" as in Leo the Lion, and others were convoluted to a whole circus of animals including, delightfully, "More-O-ver the Dog". If I now had a dog I would call him "Moreover".

Apparently the canons' merriment went too far. Eventually the then bishop, Roger de Mortival put a stop to it, pointing out that in their former isolation at Old Sarum the canons and singing vicars could meet far apart from "the tumult of laymen" disturbing them. But the new Cathedral "now lies open to all comers, some of them desirable but others undesirable". The singing had become debased and "a crowd had pressed in (not without ribaldry) for the beginning of the nine Antiphons . . . All riotous and ribald concourse" had to stop.

A document signed by Bishop Poore, the founder of the amazing enterprise, is apparently the first letter ever to be sent from the Cathedral Close. He had moved from his temporary lodgings at Mitre House, now the ladies' fashion shop outside the main gate, to his new house in The Close although he, perhaps understandably since all around him was a building site, seems unsure of the address. It is dated 28 June, 1218, and comes: "From his new place at Old Salisbury". Surely it was New Salisbury?

The house was in reality a palace, although because it was unfurnished the Bishop had difficulty in finding room for "a solemn entertainment at great expense" for the guests at the celebration of the first three altars of the Cathedral at Michaelmas 1225. The palace was enlarged and rebuilt over the years that the Cathedral was rising beside it. King Henry the Third sent ox-carts loaded with timber and today the building is a most complete and elegant memory of those days.

In 1947 the then Bishop decided that the Palace has was too big for one family and moved to the South Canonry (among other amenities "Accommodation for doves" is mentioned). The Cathedral School took over the Palace. It is strange to see now how all the bits and pieces of a school – classrooms, ranks of computers, staff quarters and studies, and the echoing toilet facilities of childhood – are somehow fitted into this fine and ancient building.

Recently I was recruited to act as narrator in a cheery sing-along production by the school of "The Sound of Music". As I stood with the professional soloists and the audience, wobblingly yodelling "The Lonely Goatherd" it came to me that the room was no ordinary assembly hall, it was the fine great drawing room of Bishop Barrington who was there in the eighteenth century. Its patterned ceiling, lovely arched Venetian windows and finely fashioned fireplace have been shown in numerous drawings and then the earliest photographs. The most noble and notable persons in the land were entertained here and now we were yodelling about this lonely goatherd, the audience jammed together on school benches and the customary knocked-about classroom chairs. I had the thought that Bishop Barrington would have enjoyed it, perhaps joined in the yodelling.

The palace is said to have been the first completed building in The Close. Sir Christopher Wren was among many, over the centuries, to have given an eye to it and to have even submitted an estimate for improvements. After "ye late troubles" as the Cromwellian era was called (and when the palace became an inn and a collection of workshops for small craftsmen) Wren put in an estimate to restore the place for "wholesome habitation" which amounted to £1,200 "and upwards" and to "finish it decently" a total of £1,500 "according to the Prices of building in that place". The eventual work, supervised not by Sir Christopher Wren but by the Cathedral clerk of works, came in under estimate at £1,140.

Deep at the bottom of the expansive house is an undercroft, so low you are tempted to crouch, where squat and massive piers confidently hold up the building above. It is still used for social functions and the Gentlemen of the Close Cricket Club, of which I was the closest resident to the pitch, (I could change into my whites and pad-up in my own home) used to hold a jolly annual dinner there. Every staircase, every ceiling, every room of this remarkable building breathes history. But try telling that to the pupils who, every day, clatter and chatter along the fabled corridors. They would probably smile politely and say "Yes".

CHAPTER 7

'I Will Assassinate the Dean'

S IR EDWARD HEATH, FORMERLY PRIME minister, had as many enemies as friends, probably more. But even today five years after his death, his name is coupled with that of his house, Arundells, and his living in The Close. Mention the location in any conversation, in any part of the country and others too, and the name "Ted Heath" will almost immediately follow. He was a character and an enigma even to those who knew him, possibly to himself.

There are only scraps of the original Close houses built by the thirteenth century canons, small piles of rubble now, and an angle of a window. But Edward Heath was proud of those ancient stones. Under the roof there are more clues than can be detected in most of the early dwellings. Smoke-blackened rafters from the open fire of a central hall are still to be seen re-used as joists in the parlour and drawing room which Ted would proudly point out as though he had discovered them in his spare time. It is not difficult to imagine those happily singing and drinking clerics of far-off nights grouped singing The Great Os while listeners who had crept from the town crowded the door. But on the right-hand flank of the garden as it runs to the river are the rough remains of an unmistakable building that echoes from those times. Whatever his pro-European outlook, Ted watched over these stones as if he were guarding them for England. He was a robust host and gave good garden parties. I recall standing on the sunny Avon bank when he introduced Diana and me to a beautiful young woman, a neighbour he had discovered, whose husband, a plastic surgeon, had been murdered by a would-be patient. Ted was frequently a sympathetic man. On that particular afternoon he finished his glass (undoubtedly malt whisky which he preferred to wine) and left his numerous guests chatting to go off and have talks with Nelson Mandella in Capetown.

Elias de Dereham, when he had a moment from masterminding the building of Salisbury Cathedral, had his own house constructed in 1220, in a design that he hoped would be followed by the canons tardily constructing theirs in The Close. Not many followed his designer wishes, it appears, which is probably just as well or what might have emerged was a prototype upper-class housing estate.

Elias built Leadenhall, which was the house on the left of

ours, and this final remnant of his thirteenth century planning was finally demolished in 1915. It was the only house in The Close built with the protection of a lead roof, hence the name.

In his copious, and occasionally inaccurate, study of historic buildings in England, Sir Nikolaus Pevsner, says that the artist John Constable spent his honeymoon in 1816 under the roof of the house which became ours in 1990, The Walton Canonry. He did not. He and Maria, his bride, spent a few days next door at Leadenhall.

Despite his enduring paintings of Salisbury Cathedral, Constable was not over-enthusiastic about Wiltshire. The East Anglian, used to famously widespread vistas and fine open light, thought of Salisbury as "muggy". He sat, in 1820, on the Avon bank opposite the garden of Leadenhall (which he refers to as 'Leydenhall'), and worked on a landscape which has a rich country thickness about it. It finds the Cathedral (not without a minor shifting it seems) in a gap between Leadenhall where he was a guest and our house. It is one of his most noteworthy works and yet when it came before the Hanging Committee of the Royal Academy was rejected for exhibition. And John Constable, by that time in full fame, was a member of that committee.

Guides in the Cathedral today set a quiz question for tourists: Spot the difference in one of the carved figures of Bishops above the choir stalls. They are shiny wood and refer to ages darker than they are. The answer is that one bishop from the 16th century is not wearing his mitre. This is to signify that

Cardinal Laurence Campeggio, the last Catholic bishop, never actually came to Salisbury at all, preferring to send messages from Rome. The house allotted to him, Aula le Stage, the House with the Tower, can be seen today at the corner of the delightfully shy Rosemary Lane in The Close. The man I knew who lived there in our time had a name that could have come from the radio series "The Archers" – Walter Partridge. His grandfather, with wife and thirteen children, had been summarily ejected from their Norfolk cottage because he would not tell his employer the name of the candidate he intended to vote for in an election. The local vicar came around to act as bailiff, to make sure they went. The family went sorrowfully away in a borrowed cart. Walter was a shiny eyed, wiry little man, who became a master printer and, when I knew him, lived in Aula le Stage with a printing press and his dear wife Betty. He tried (without success) to teach me to fish.

Every ancient house in The Close has its story. There were dramas and romances. Half the history of England passed through the stone arches and the famous and infamous slept below the carved ceilings. Some were characters, some brave, some beautiful; some were distinct oddities. The Canon who once lived in what became Sir Edward Heath's house, Arundells, was ejected for "practising majick".

Hemyngsby, one of the first houses to be constructed by those builder-churchmen, housed a canon called Nicholas Upton who was at the side of the Earl of Salisbury when the

Earl was killed fighting Joan of Arc's army at Orleans in 1428. New occupiers of most of the properties were obliged to take part in a sort of celestial game of Monopoly. It was called Obits and required the player who wished to live in a certain house to pay a set sum of money every year to finance prayers for the previous owner's soul. Failure to do so and any further financial irregularities could perhaps end with a sort of "Go to Gaol" sentence.

In 1547, after the Reformation, Simon Symonds, the famous Vicar of Bray, arrived with his chattels. He was the man who boasted of his powers of survival no matter who was on the throne or which politician was in power. He changed his coat more readily than he changed his vestments and they even sang a song about him: "No matter the king who reigns in the land, I'm still the vicar of Bray!" Apparently he remained so. How or why he became the resident of Hemyngsby is not apparent. For all his fame in Bray, on the Thames, he appears to have been a non-entity in Salisbury Cathedral Close, quite an achievement for a notorious man.

Then there was John Farrant who tried to assassinate the Dean. Known for his rages, he had always been a troublesome man, an odd choice for a "Moderator", one of the most senior among the lower Cathedral clergy. Once he had been involved in a fist fight in the churchyard with a Lay-Vicar, Christopher Cranborne, both wearing their vestments. Farrant was a man who dwelt darkly on matters and he was convinced that Dean Bridges was trying to get rid of him, which may have been true. So, on a Saturday in 1591, anyone near the Cathedral would have been intrigued to see an obviously irate clergyman rushing from the afternoon service with a billowing cassock and a puce face. Under the cassock was a long knife and Farrant intended to use it on the Dean. He was followed by a chorister, probably shouting "Stop! Stop!", a seventeen year old called William Deane. Farrant, at the end of the second lesson, had called him to follow and, mouthing threats, set out from the West Door towards the old Deanery.

The youth, in his evidence to the inevitable inquiry, described the rush across the churchyard and how he went to Dr. Bridges to tell him that Farrant was after him. The Dean, who was in his study, told them to go away because he was busy. "By God I will speak with thee!" Farrant shouted. Then Deane described what followed: ". . . going into the studie in furious and angry sorte threw off his surplice and his gown and stepping to Dr. Bridges took him by the collar of his gown and said: 'Thou goest to take away my living, but, God's Wounds, Ile cutt thy throat'". Dr. Bridges eventually escaped, leaving his tattered gown in Farrant's grasp. With remarkable aplomb Farrant, followed by the confused and frightened youth, then left the house, went across the churchyard to the Cathedral where they picked up their books and continued with the afternoon service.

⁓

Farrant was soon dismissed but apparently got another job at Hereford Cathedral, leaving behind his circumspect son, also

John Farrant, who became the organist at Salisbury and served the Cathedral for eighteen blameless years.

For half-a-century a choral group called The Farrant Singers has been popular in Salisbury and elsewhere. They were bravely named, not after John Farrant, the decent son who was organist at the Cathedral for eighteen years, but after his miscreant father who, among other things, drew a knife on the Dean. The father went from cathedral to cathedral after that, always leaving under a deep shadow.

"Our choral group was named after him, John Farrant the elder," explains the historian Julian Wiltshire stoutly – "Because he was a truly great organist."

CHAPTER 8

Dora Opens the Door

IN THE MID-NINETEEN-TWENTIES a remarkable woman appeared in Salisbury Close. Single and singular, her name was Dora H. Butterworth and she arrived, having taken the appropriate diplomas, to become matron of the Cathedral School. She fell in love with the school, with the choirboy pupils – and with the headmaster. She and Arthur G. Robertson, who she always respectfully called AGR, were married in October 1925. He was a widower of fifty-seven, but according to his demonstratively smitten bride he was more like a man of forty in appearance and high spirits. Six feet one and a half inches tall (her description is precise) "magnified by cassock and gown into something colossal, with whirlwind movements, red hair, a great laugh and a ringing voice". He was a crackshot with an airgun and could unerringly pick off a water-rat on the far bank of the Avon. He played bagatelle and billiards, could knock up a forceful 50 at cricket and, she adds with a quaint innocence, "a few moments later could be massaging the small and sensitive tummy of a little boy who feels sick".

The headmaster taught photography and other hobbies, sometimes gave object lessons in "how to masticate" and knew about boat repairs. His coaching methods were the making of the cricket team (at practice a batsman's right foot was tethered to the ground by a leather thong) and Festival matches were played by the older boys against even the large, rough and aggressive soldiers of the Bulford Military Garrison.

But legendary as AGR became, his star was unknowingly eclipsed by the endeavours of his wife Dora. It was she who opened the creaking door of the Munument Room of the Cathedral Archives where the documents of centuries were rolled and stored, the Chapter Acts Books and Registers, Accounts of Finances and ancient leases which had scarcely been studied since the day they were signed.

She was helped by willing local scholars led by Canon Christopher Wordsworth, who translated (for the first time in many instances) the Latin words. What was gradually revealed was a treasure trove going back six hundred years. Because of the aptly named Wordsworth and the enthusiastic Dora, doubtless egging him on, much of the early story of Salisbury Cathedral is open to our eyes. Nor was Dora shy of presenting her characters with all their warts: "Here are the young Vicars, half-priests, half body-servants of the Canons, filling the Close with their brawls, insulting the Close Porter, practising archery, playing tennis, keeping too many dogs, singing in the taverns of the town, conducting their amours with the citizens' wives, fooling with the Choristers during service."

She had opened a can of Cathedral worms.

For all the piety and the prayers, the chanting of the hours by day and the vespers at night, for all the orders of service and precedence, there was an unholy whiff of violence revealed by the records of those early days. Apart from merely local disputes and crimes , vicious as they often were, there was almost a war between Salisbury clergy and those at York which had to thank a considerable width of No-mans-land that it did not become more bloody.

The Salisbury contingent was led by two brothers, successive Precentors of the church, who were beyond doubt scoundrels. Boniface and George de Saluzzo were church appointments because of noble birth, and were a pair not so much wedded to God as to utter lawlessness. They do not seem to have opened the letter from the Pope informing them of their ex-communication and proceeded with both their religious and disreputable ways.

During the dispute with York the brothers ambushed the Rural Dean of Pontefract, who was coming south to try and talk them out of an armed invasion of the northern diocese, having been sent by the Archbishop. They almost beat the life out of the reverend messenger carrying the placatory letter, then cut the ears and tails off the mules transporting the York party before sending them packing.

On his return to Salisbury, news of his ex-communication having apparently been ignored or not received, Boniface succeeded his brother as Precentor of the Cathedral whose job was the well-being of the choirboys.

It was a sword-edged age. William Longespee, Earl of Salisbury, who had laid one of the foundation stones of the Cathedral (his wife, the lovely and noble Countess Ela laid another) was probably murdered in an off-guard moment.

He was one of England's most illustrious men, the natural son of King Henry the Second, his mother described by the chroniclers of the time as the "fair Rosamond" de Clifford. He married Ela, Countess of Salisbury in her own right, when she was twelve years of age. His half-brothers were the notorious King John and the exalted Richard Coeur de Lion.

Longespee spent much of his life looking for a fight. He would battle with anyone, anywhere, by land or sea. He stopped several invasions of England in their tracks. One of his notable victories was against a French fleet commanded by a vile-tempered pirate called Eustace the Monk.

He was away from home, at some war or other, for years. In action against the French he was struck unconscious by a massive blow delivered by the Bishop of Beauvais wielding his ceremonial mace. Taken prisoner he was sportingly exchanged and went home to Ela. Soon he was campaigning again. News came that he had been lost at sea. The desirable and wealthy Countess was widowed so everyone believed –

except her. A minor nobleman arrived at her door, dressed in finery above his pocket, and proposed marriage to her but she sniffily turned him away. "Seek elsewhere for a wife," said Ela. She still believed that Longespee would come home, and come home he did. He had been held up on a voyage from Western France – for three months.

Angrily he went looking for "the twerp" Raymond de Burgh, who had propositioned his wife, and having found him extracted gifts of valuable horses. The Countess was worth a good many horses. Then he made his naive and fatal mistake. He accepted De Burgh's invitation to dinner, of all things, and within two days became ill and died. After all his battles the fatal blow was delivered at the table.

He was the first man to be buried in the Cathedral he helped to found. Ela took herself off to establish Lacock Abbey and lived there in wisdom and widowhood for the rest of her life. She outlived three of her four sons.

The mystery of her husband's death is still unsolved. Centuries after he was buried with pomp in Salisbury Cathedral his tomb was opened – and *two* skeletons were found. One was the Earl, the other was a rat. The bones of the rat were *inside* the skull of the nobleman.

Was Longespee poisoned and did he then, grimly in death, poison the foraging rat?

No one now will ever know.

CHAPTER 9

'Verie Lowsey' Choirboys

ON THE FRONT OF MY present house in the Liberty of Salisbury Cathedral Close – the area surrounding The Close and having the same rules and rights – there is a carving of an angel. He is not your usual angelic angel, although he has folded golden wings. But there is an urchin look about him, snubbed nose and curly hair. He carries a blue and white coat of arms and an open book. He was here when I bought the house two years ago and no one seems to know who put him on the wall.

My neighbour, the Reverend Jeremy Ames, who is not keen on religious trappings says, with dismissive ex-Royal Navy phraseology: "He's just a gash angel". But at the College of Arms in London no less a person than Pursuivant Rouge Dragon wrote to tell me my angel bears the Arms of

Oxford University, rarely seen displayed outside the University City.

The angel's reference goes back, however mistily, to the French connection with Salisbury in 1260 when some religious students from the Auverne fled their settlement under duress and arrived, doubtless with relief, into The Close. Wild as life was in the Cathedral and the town in those times (Salisbury was the tenth most populated city in Britain), immigrants are not always too particular and the students gladly settled themselves in a corner of The Close. In France their settlement had been called Home of the Scholars of the Valley and the new one took the name The College of De Vaux. My house, some stones of it anyway, are the remains of that college.

The French were joined at some time by students fleeing Oxford, either from the not infrequent outbreaks of the plague or from the consequences of University high spirits. Three Oxford students were hanged after "accidentally killing a woman" and another group left hurriedly after killing a Master of Cooks who had outraged them by throwing hot greasy water in the face of a begging priest. They were unruly times.

The De Vaux College has some claim to being the first residential university college in England. Its charter, still to be read in the Cathedral library, says that the House of the Valley Scholars established in a meadow near the Cathedral would forever house "twenty poor needy honest and docile scholars . . .". And one woman. How Christina Moton ever got into the celibate establishment is a mystery. But, together with her benefactor husband she was set at the students' table and given a chamber of her own. Her husband was given a place to keep his horse.

The ghost of Christina is said to roam the house today. The staff of the Sarum Partnership, the Cathedral Architects, who once occupied the buildings, reported seeing her standing behind the mullioned windows, waving sadly as someone who does not hope to get a friendly response. She has not shown herself to us during our time in residence but, with its beams, chimneys and puzzling corners, its panelling and the huge 15th century oak beam over the open fireplace the scene looks to be set. One night, one day, perhaps . . .

The noble Cathedral, built with skill, devotion and imagination that approached genius had by the fifteen hundreds unbelievably, begun to decay. It was like Gulliver, kept captive by pygmies, and neglectful pygmies at that, as though a visible miracle was being shrugged off.

The canons of the time, appointed by Rome, were rarely in attendance. Although drawing their stipends some never visited Salisbury, or even England, once. The fine fabric was beginning to moulder, the singing faltered, the prayers were gabbled, nobody cleaned the windows and the pigeons came back to roost. A horse fair – and all that meant -was held in the Cathedral itself. The money was dwindling, the houses which the first canons had been ordered to build in The Close were falling down and the graveyard which surrounded the great church was becoming increasingly gruesome. Sheep and cows jostled for bits of grass in what had been the "fair meadow" and the river was clogged with mud and weeds. Salisbury was a downcast place. What clergy were in evidence could not be adequately paid, there was insufficient food on the tables but the beer flowed well enough in the taverns of the town.

Neglect was everywhere but nowhere more apparent than in the state of the Cathedral choirboys. They had been for generations, quite literally, the whipping boys. Summoned from bed on cruel winter's nights with a stroke of the master's rod to troop to the unheated Cathedral to sing early morning praises, their cassocked ranks had dwindled by the early sixteen hundreds (at one time they numbered just six). Successive singing masters tried to ignore their responsibility and the boys' food, clothing and general well-being came bottom of the list in the struggling community.

Choirboys, crouched like little old men, could be seen begging at street corners in a city that had been helped to commercial prosperity and a considerable measure of fame by the Cathedral where they were supposed to be singing. After a near riot, an investigation of their diet was held and, in what must have been a Dickensian scene years before Dickens, masters sampled the mouldy bread and sour beer which just kept the boys alive. Some improvements may have resulted but they are not recorded. The children relied in many cases on the pity of the townspeople. Patience among these solid folk became limited and they protested to the Dean and Chapter that the boys' treatment had resulted in them becoming "verie lowsey". They had to be taken and hosed down, scrubbed, de-loused and re-clothed. Salisbury people were outraged at these "foule defects". The processions through the nave had been walked by boys in "ragged sluttish and uncleanly surplices" to the shame of those who were supposed to care for them.

⌒✐⌒

Even with the occasional pity of strangers, a piece of cloth to make a coat, a cap for winter, an extra ration of suspect bread, the lot of the young singers did not improve. Individual benefits accrued and some of these seem to have been overlooked entirely in the mish-mash times. Funds left to comfort the rough lives of the young choirboys sometimes mysteriously turned up to finance something the canons wanted more. One legacy was counted out in the Chapter House with great ceremony. The boys' eyes must have glistened but it was eight years until the first few coins of interest came their way. It took generations for matters to improve although they did eventually, even to the extent of the Cathedral funding the occasional choristers' outing to Salisbury Races. The races – which are still regularly run – began in 1585 when the Earl of Pembroke donated a golden bell, worth £50 it was noted, to start the horses. Muskets were fired at every mile post.

As resourceful children, the boys made their own fun, swinging, trapezing perilously high in the tall shadows of the tower and the nave. They were proud of these gymnastics, so much so that two of the best performers, eager to show off to a royal visitor, both tried one leap too far and fell to their deaths. The details of the tragedy, even the names of the victims, seem to have been erased or lost.

There was always cock-fighting. In better times some choristers owned fierce and truculent birds and set them on each other's necks in one of the classrooms of the Cathedral School. This often developed into fighting between the owners.

On the icy winter days there was also skating on the water meadows and on the frozen Avon and games which included jousting-at-speed, the participants charging at each other across the iced-up river. The school was never heated, nor was the Cathedral, but the singers tried to keep warm with activity. They captured birds in the roof of the Cathedral and kept them in cages in their classrooms. At Christmas small clutches of choirboys muttered cold carols while holding begging bowls under the not always sympathetic noses of local citizens. There were later a few bonuses; horsemen who entered the Cathedral still wearing their spurs were fined "spur money" by the nearest choirboy and usually paid up, as did the illustrious Duke of Wellington in later times. Running games were played, often to the chanting of not very holy versions of the psalms, along the toothy stone ramparts of the surrounding wall, another fruitful source of casualties. But one of the more unusual, some would say bizarre, activities was the church-inspired festival of the Boy Bishop.

In the nave today, placed among the worn procession of solemnly sleeping tombstones, is a child-sized effigy which is by tradition the grave of a boy-bishop who presumably died when at the height of his briefly imposed fame, but is more likely to hold the heart of an adult, a cleric who is buried elsewhere.

It is still introduced by the guide as "the reputed boy

bishop" and it recalls the fantasy of an elected chorister, arrayed in finery to match that of the real bishop, carried in procession, leading a service, and fêted by his fellows. Being juveniles, the fêting often got out of hand and there were catcalls and raucous singing as the chosen boy processed down the aisle. Objects were thrown. In the end the church put an end to it (although there are moves to revive it), the ribaldry had to cease and the boy bishop reverted to being just another singing lad with a tough life.

CHAPTER 10

The Vulgar Vicars

TODAY IT MIGHT EVEN BE likened to an ecclesiastical rat race; the tight society was strictly graded from the bishop to the lowliest piping choirboy, but it was much harder for the choirboy to progress towards heaven, or even the better situations available on earth.

Reading through the translations of Canon Wordsworth, the originals still to be seen in the curled archives of the Munument Room, the headmaster's wife, Dora Robertson, in her nineteen thirties account "Sarum Close" forsakes her customary fair and mild rebuke for the situation by bluntly saying: ". . . this state of affairs between fellow priests serving the same cathedral has proved a running sore in the whole history of the Church of Sarum".

At the bottom of the pile (except, of course, for the

choirboys) were the Vicars Choral. There were forty of them, clerical dogsbodies whose main function seemed not far short of making up the numbers at services. They were scarcely more than youths who had memorised every holy note. They had to sing at all services, day and night, and stand-in for the canons when they were absent on business, had a hangover or had gone off hunting.

They were not highly regarded in the church due to their considerable lack of devotion and discipline; some might be described as louts in cassocks. They were only one step above the wretched choirboys – literally, since places in the choir were severely designated and their step was raised only a few inches above the rugged boy singers. As a penance for any uncovered misdeeds they would be ordered to sing on the step *below* the choir or made to go without several dinners. There seems to have been a distinct lack of Christian love.

These Vicars Choral came into being in the middle of the fourteenth century and were soon the centre of trouble. More than a few of the Statutes of Salisbury Cathedral, as translated by Canon Wordsworth, concern complaints about the Vicars Choral and the punishments imposed on them.

They were dismissed as "Slanderers, flatterers, buffoons and backbiters" who "dispising to undergo the toil to which man is born, look for a living in ease and laziness". Worse was to follow: "they were called in the vulgar speech *minstrels and players*" and, among other restrictions, they were not allowed to purchase bread if sold by a woman. Difficult times indeed. Despite these shortcomings, the Vicars Choral were allowed in the houses of the clergy but to be given nothing which could be turned into money by these "upholders of sloth and all the vices"

When they were on frequent duty in the Cathedral, the Vicars Choral were also warned that they must abstain from quarrelling, laughing and mocking. Nor, when attending any services should they indulge in "running hither and thither . . . nor leaping and skipping . . .". These athletic sins were apparently repeated in Salisbury itself and the Statute makes a point of it; "We do ordain and command that the Vicars of our church go not running about the streets and squares of the town". And especially not alone: . . . "lest perchance they fall and have none to raise them up."

Despite their obvious poverty the Vicars Choral were, they hoped, lively young men of fashion. The vestments of the church they were obliged to wear every day (and which were often hand-downs from the canons who employed them) were quickly thrown off at every opportunity and they headed for the taverns and streets of Salisbury, looking for drink, women and adventure, dressed to the nines. And very odd nines they appear to have been – including the extraordinary parsnip boots of the day, tapering several inches beyond the toes and patterned in red and green squares. Men of fashion wore these. There is a drawing of the city's most powerful and wealthy man, Sir John Hall, splay footed, his shoes extending far beyond his toes.

When the Vicars Choral began to ape these extravagances, the first action taken by the Cathedral authorities was to utterly ban all forms of flamboyant dress. One Vicar,

Adam Gore, a trouble maker who appears regularly in the bad books of the church, was charged "that he walks day by day in the Close and in the City in a short and light coat, encircled with a belt of marvellous size contrary to the honesty of his order." There is no mention of his "marvellous" shoes. He was ordered to wear decent and sufficient habit. It may be that Adam was as much sinned against as sinning. He attracted more trouble in 1394 for singing flat in church although he was not the only one; there was squabbling in the choir and a shirking of funerals.

Several of these supposed holy youths gained a sinful reputation with women. John Rede was an enthusiastic seducer and often brawled with his love rivals. His arch enemy, Richard Gidy, was exposed as having a child by a lady in the town "one Agnes".

The antics of another Vicar, John Hullying, caused a riot in Salisbury when the Mayor and a crowd of townspeople marched on the Chapter accusing Hullying of having a long relationship with a woman aptly named Constance. He protested that he had only paused at her house for a few hours on his way to Wells. The house was only a short distance from where he was accommodated in The Close but he thought he might as well rest there before he set out on his journey. He seems to have wriggled out of that one but, according to the translated statutes, he was in further trouble later for shouting out loud during Divine Service and singing with "approbious and contumelious words" to disrupt the worship.

There were worse crimes. John Homyngton, a chaplain, was murdered and robbed. No accused was named in the records, but a Vicar called John Babestoke walked through the Cathedral, The Close and town, armed with a dagger "which he often drew against his fellows". Once, this happened a few minutes after the evening service while the attacked cleric was returning innocently to his house, perhaps mulling over the sermon.

CHAPTER 11

Dean and Double Agent

IN THE SPRING OF 1943, when the Second World War was occupying the world, an academic American lady was sitting in the silence of her university library researching and writing about a man of whom few people had ever heard.

John Gordon was a double-dealing, double agent, born 299 years before. Dr. Dorothy Quynn was uncovering the life of a confidence trickster, a fraud, a blatant liar, a spy – and Dean of Salisbury Cathedral. Anyone looking at her papers now might come to the conclusion that the lady academic's own story was only slightly less fascinating than the sly man she was investigating. She had pursued her quarry through Scotland and England and into many corners of France. She may have initiated these journeys prior to the start of the war in 1939. On the other hand it is tempting to think, bearing in mind the complicated and, to her compelling nature of the story, that perhaps she pottered about France, notebook and pencil in hand, while the battles were going on around her, perhaps even during the German invasion in the summer of 1940, when the United States was neutral and Americans could still travel (with difficulty and bravery) to France. Perhaps she continued following the trail *even during the first year of the occupation*. America did not enter the war until the Pearl Harbour attack in December 1941 and neutral U.S. citizens could visit German-conquered France and some did. It is tempting to picture Dr. Quynn, notebook in hand, ferreting through French libraries and record offices while the German occupiers watched her with surprise and suspicion.

The object of her detective work, John Gordon, was once depicted on a memorial brass in Salisbury Cathedral, but this only adds another mystery because this has now disappeared. A counter-proof reproduction can be seen at the British Museum, a bearded man supported by angels, holding up both hands as if to say: "I didn't do it". He lived with his second wife (having apparently forgotten a first family) in The Close mixing with the Cathedral high life of his day including Dr. Richard Haydocke, a physician there for forty years, who was rumoured to give sermons in his sleep.

Gordon was from a Scottish family, his father having been Bishop of Galloway and, poetically, Abbot of Tongland. In the chaotic religious upheavals of the times, when clerics changed sides more often than they changed their vestments, his father was deposed from his status, but somehow hung onto the intrinsic revenues. John Gordon's story is of spending years just running ahead of the truth. He connived and plotted within the triangle of the French Court, Queen Elizabeth the First and Mary Queen of Scots. His manoeuvres gained him favours and semi-recognition but no faction ever quite believed him.

The burrowing Dr. Quynn set out her indictment in an article published in 'The Historian' at Arizona State University in the autumn of 1943. Half a century later Ralph B. Weller, a Salisbury historian, added his own conclusions in a treatise 'The Strange Case of John Gordon Double-Agent and Dean of Salisbury'.

Gordon spent many years hovering around the French Court, with secret forays into the worlds of Queen Elizabeth of England and Mary Queen of Scots, making much of his supposed connections and spying one against the other, although in truth few people seemed to be quite sure who he was or cared much what he was up to. He fiercely believed his own importance and spent much time spelling it out in letters to the highest in three lands. The spelling, however, was weak.

Those were dangerous days and John Gordon blithely lied and sidled his way between factions, supping with one and dining with another, as one politician noted, and going home clutching money from both. "A very false merchant indeed" observed Henry Killigrew, the English ambassador to Scotland.

Astonishingly, Gordon was only thrown into prison once and then emerged after no great time with his head still attached to his shoulders.

He was in the habit of peppering his many letters with what

appeared to be learned phrases from classic languages, Hebrew, Arabic and Ethiopian among them. The politicians of the day doubtless raised their eyebrows. It took the assiduous Dorothy M. Quynn, centuries later, to detect that these impressive additions were utterly fraudulent. Twentieth century scholars needed little more than a glance to see that these learned sentiments, in remote tongues, were meaningless, merely picked up at random and written into the letter to give the impression of advanced education which few people, even in high places, could disprove. It was akin to appending some slogan like "Come to Ethiopia for your Holidays" or "Camels for Sale in Damascus" at random to the letters. Gordon's Ethiopian effusions were proved to be ungrammatical and often devoid of point, written by someone who had simply copied them from another context.

Like a literary bloodhound, Dr. Quynn tracked down a tale by Gordon, which he had sent in detail to half the politicians and nobility in Europe, and she demolished it word by word as fantasy. It was supposed to have happened at Avignon during its pre-eminence as a Roman Catholic centre, and involved important figures within any number of churches. Dr. Quynn (in the middle of a 20th Century World War, remember) revealed that its date was wrong, this cleric was not born, that there never had been a rabbi called Benetrius . . . She had rifled through the French State Archives page by page and once more proved the future Dean of Salisbury was making it up.

Luck remained steadfastly at John Gordon's elbow. It patted his shoulder encouragingly once more when King James the Fourth of Scotland became James the First of England, after the death of Queen Elizabeth. James was a slightly distant kinsman and Gordon was promptly installed as Dean of Salisbury. He became Dean in February 1604 and remained so until his death on 3 September 1619, living with his wife in The Close but often away on uncertain business. Even in death there was room for doubt, two differing dates for his demise are given in various documents, bequests in his will, one in favour of the choirboys, were never carried out and the Cloisters are still awaiting the rebuilding he proposed to finance.

Dorothy M. Quynn drives in her last nail with the observation that John Gordon fails to mention his first family in France in his will and indeed refers to "my onlie child" being in England. She suspects that the Dean of Salisbury managed to keep his two families in total ignorance of each other – the final lie in a life full of deception.

Who stole his brass memorial from the Cathedral has never been known. Perhaps it was his ghost.

CHAPTER 12

A Spinster Spins Out of Control

DOWN ALL THE CENTURIES OF their history Salisbury Cathedral and its famous Close have been the concerns of the male sex. From Bishops to bricklayers it is men who have shaped their twin destinies. Men have written tens of thousands of words about these unusual places. And yet the three most human accounts of what happened there have been fashioned by women. Male clerks and Canons may have pieced together the dry accounts, the ledgers and the diaries but the warmth and humour of what life really was like in that island space is contained in the story-telling of three diverse women, Dora Robertson with her caring history of the choir and the colourful clergy, translated for her from the original documents in the nineteen-thirties; the American scholar Dr. Dorothy Quynn and her painstaking detection in the matter of the suspicious and shadowy Dean, John Gordon, and its deep insight into those turbulent times as I have just related; and a gloriously different lady, Miss Frances Child and her late nineteenth century tale 'The Spinster at Home in the Close of Salisbury'.

Miss Child's book is a jig saw of poetry; a jig saw where the pieces fit only approximately, a serious rival to the aching work of her near-contemporary William McGonagall. She sets out her stall early:

> *"Mine's a tiny abode well-befitting a Spinster*
> *In a nook of the Close ever claimed by its Minister"*

From this nook she recorded every manner of Close life, being particularly keen on ghosts, ghastly murders and royal visits.

> *"Of all kinds of murthe, here's a Canto brimful*
> *Which, from various sources I've laboured to cull"*

She would never allow a difficult rhyme get in her way. Relating the bloodthirsty end of the Duke of Buckingham in 1483 at the behest of King Richard the Third on the site off Salisbury's market square, now occupied by Debenham's store, she was at her most imaginative:

> *"Richard sent up to London*
> *The Duke of Buckingham's right arm and head . . .*
> *Two most bloody mementos to scare all the cits*
> *Out of their wits."*

Miss Child sharpened her quill to recall the visit of the Duke and Duchess of Kent with their infant Victoria.

> *"Though 'tis long since in Salisbury a monarch resided*
> *And betwixt this and Windsor such honour divided,*
> *Royal visitants hither when travelling or drawn*
> *By the fame of the church and its fair verdant lawn*
> *The month of December, eighteen hundred and twenty*
> *Brought Kent's Duke and Duchess with high nobles and gentry*
> *And their infant Victoria, our present great Queen*
> *Who by all ranks and ages was most eagerly seen . . ."*

Few of the ranks escaped her descriptive assaults:

> *"Earls Radnor and Pembroke show their beautiful seats . . ."*

Recently, in the Salisbury Museum, a pair of Queen Victoria's bloomers was exhibited as part of a display of the garments of former days. They had a fifty-one inch waist. Surveying them I had an uncomfortable feeling accentuated when I read in The Times that they were later auctioned in London. (They fetched £4,500. Sold to a collector – a collector?) Surely a delayed instance of *lèse-majestè*.

Queen Victoria had visited Salisbury only sparsely. The peon penned by the redoubtable Spinster of The Close, Frances Child, was her first time. (What a brave poet was Miss Child. Even the outrageously great McGonagall would not have attempted to rhyme "wits" with "cits".)

Some monarchs favoured Salisbury more than others. King James the First could hardly stay away. He gave us, in the Liberty of The Close, as well as the people of The Close itself, a grim charter including the right to utilise a set of gallows, with stocks and whipping post, established in the Cathedral grounds and the key to le Grate - a small prison. A lavatory and some pig sties were also to be removed. It gave a new aspect to the surroundings. So often was King James lodging in The Close that a statue of him was fitted into the niche over the main gate in place of that of Henry the Third which was falling to pieces, so decayed the King could have been anybody. Then during the sixteen hundreds, in an age when it was not unknown for monarchs to literally lose their heads, James' stone head was removed and that of Charles the First attached to his father's body. There it remained until early in the 20th century when the man of several parts was removed altogether and the entire (although scarcely wholesome) figure of King Edward the Seventh replaced it. He is still there, still in one piece.

King James the Second overstayed his time in The Close and paid for it with his throne. On November 18th, 1688, under threat from William of Orange, he rode into Salisbury with his troops. Greeted as usual with municipal joy he was then gripped by a nose-bleed that lasted two days. When it was at last stemmed he set off for Windsor but only got as far as Hungerford.

In the meantime, William of Orange and his army arrived and the Mayor and burghers of Salisbury pragmatically greeted him with all the colour and ceremony which they had afforded King James only days before. Then, William and his men set off to eventually claim the crown.

The frequency of royal visits had always put a financial strain on the people of Salisbury who were expected to dress in their best, leave their employment and wave to order. Muddy roads had to be covered in gravel and beggars dragged from the streets and hidden.

Then there was a cavalcade of leading citizens, the aldermen (twenty-four of them) arrayed in scarlet, leading the way followed by forty-eight councillors in violet and black. Whole swathes of citizens decked themselves in green. There were pages and heralds and an army of tradesmen in distinctive colours and on horseback, the horses being hung with coloured bunting. If the royal person arrived after dark every street in the city was lit by torches and flaming barrels. It was a fine sight, but expensive. Apart from the ceremonial handing over of the keys of the gates, and the Mayor's mace (which was, at least, given back to him) there was a tariff which the visitor expected to pocket. A silver cup costing twenty pounds and containing gold coins to the value of another twenty was the customary gift to a king; then a Queen would get a purse harbouring another twenty pounds. And it all came out of the rates.

King Henry the Eighth came twice with different wives: first Katherine of Aragon and later with Anne Boleyn who was given a present (or a fee perhaps) amounting to twenty pounds, three shillings and fourpence.

As the reigns went on, the value of the monetary gifts, of course, increased. The Salisbury treasurer's heart must have often dipped. A hundred guineas was presented to King George the First when he had hardly set foot over the city boundary. And there were fifty guineas for the Prince of Wales who arrived with him. But the King did make gifts to the local deserving causes (except that of the city coffers), including the Cathedral and Workhouse. He also paid up the debts of people behind bars for owing money. There were plenty and it cost the King £1,758. 11s.

The Duke of Kent favoured the West Country which had become a destination to escape the icy winters of the capital. Weymouth and Sidmouth with their mild sea air were popular but soon discovered to be fickle destinations. After the customary extravagant welcome to The Close, the Duke was brought back within a few days in a coffin. He had been out in the Sidmouth snow and had become so engrossed on his return indoors in playing with his small daughter that he had omitted to take off his cold, wet boots. He died of pleurisy.

The royal visits continued. Special banquets had to be laid on, sumptuous chambers prepared, and, at periods when the Cathedral choir was depleted through hard times, singers and musicians had to be transported in stage coaches and on horseback from Windsor and Winchester, paid and accommodated. The city treasurer must have dreaded the occasions. Once, a monarch turned up, all but unexpectedly, with *six* princesses and a prince, doubtless looking forward to their share of the Salisbury bounty.

CHAPTER 13

The Battle of Salisbury

Fighting in Salisbury has historically been between the townspeople, or the clergy, or the townspeople versus the clergy. Combatants were not confined to the male sex. In Britford parish records is an entry from ~August 1st, 1653: "A woman slayne in the Fair with a box given her on the ear, died and was buried in this churchyard: the woman striking was hanged." In the normal sense of a military battle there has only been one and that was little more than a skirmish with farcical overtones, and an edge of tragedy.

Although it has a always been surrounded by military towns and camps and, although the great Salisbury Plain, scattered with soldiers and sheep, rises dark just beyond its boundaries the city has never had a garrison nor a barracks which, perhaps, is the reason that any warlike action has been kept at an arm's distance. Even today it is rare to see uniformed servicemen in the streets, except when they are marching to or from some special church parade at the Cathedral and the inhabitants turn out to watch them go by. Troops just returned from Iraq marched to the Cathedral only recently. My grandson, Joe, watched them swinging their arms as they marched. He was shocked. "Most of them are just kids." He said. He is twenty-three.

During the Second World War the tower below the spire of the Cathedral was the nightly base for fire-watchers waiting to raise the alarm should one small incendiary bomb fall on the roof. A fire engine was permanently stationed below. And yet there was no damage, or little beyond the cluster of bullet holes in two of the copper globes of the cross that was on top of the spire. It was taken down and placed in the Cathedral. Who knows which side, which gunner, was responsible for them.

From their high posts, however, the fire watchers could clearly see Southampton blazing twenty miles away as the German bombers targeted the docks. Every evening there were reverse commuters leaving the trains from Southampton at Salisbury Station, carrying bedrolls and tents and children, returning in the morning to see if they could find their homes amid the rubble.

War touched the city and The Close in other ways, of course. Lieutenant Tom Adlam, once a pupil at Bishop Wordsworth's School, won the Victoria Cross on the Somme in World War One and the famous artist Rex Whistler, who lived in my house before me, was killed a few weeks after D-Day in Normandy. Admiral Teddy Gueritz, the famous beach-master at that invasion, has just died in The Close.

Some of the houses, and the Cathedral itself, have been used to contain war prisoners. A captured Dutch soldier, confined within the inescapable walls of the Cloisters, a handy place for a prison camp, missed his cat so much that he carved its likeness in the masonry. You can see it there today.

∼ᴍ∽

The Cathedral and its Close survived the English Civil War without the deep damage suffered by Lichfield and Worcester and even neighbouring Winchester. The lack of a garrison and fortifications saved it. But there had been early rumblings. The trading town, like most of its kind, settled for Cromwell's Parliamentarians, despite its anxious enthusiasm for royal visitors over the years, quickly restored after the Commonwealth was replaced. Salisbury people were adept at changing their coats.

But feelings swelled before the civil war began. In 1633 a local man Henry Sherfield smashed a stained glass window in St. Edmund's Church because, he said, he was annoyed by the image of God as "a little old man in a blue and red coat". His defence in court was even more fanciful. He had broken the window, he pleaded, to let in more light, so that the congregation could better read their prayer books. He was heavily fined after the judge said that any alterations in churches had to be sanctioned by the bishop. People should not go into churches to "make batteries at glass windows at their pleasure".

When the civil war began there were plenty of weapons in the city; pikes and axes and swords, and a man called Braithwaite enthusiastically made available twelve prime muskets for the Puritan cause, although whether he ever got them back is not recorded. In the Cathedral the baubles and relics were hidden as much as possible. The clergy were on the Royalists' side. Salisbury, however, was famous for its wavering and there were times when no one knew who was a friend and who a foe. George Tennum, who lived in the town, was condemned by the authorities for allowing his wife to sew and his daughter to knit on the Sabbath. Smiling was frowned upon. But Salisbury Races were held as usual.

The citizens outside the enclave of The Close were well-armed but nervous about fighting. The Mayor mustered a band of would-be soldiers but neither he nor they had any inkling of military training. There would be casualties, quite a lot of them, from what we know today as friendly fire.

Armies, or parts of them, came and went. The Royalists put the Mayor behind bars in his own prison. In the summer of 1644 a Parliamentary detachment, backing away from the enemy, was mocked by some people who had already changed sides several times. Its commanding officer stopped the retreat and fined all those onlookers who had laughed at his troops.

King Charles the First himself was at the head of 11,000 soldiers passing through the city. He left some men behind and once the main force had marched off Parliamentary general Edmund Ludlow broke cover and his men attacked the Royalists who shut themselves in The Close, only to be captured after the gates had been burned down.

The Battle of Salisbury followed a few months later. Military engagements, of any age in history, have frequently been a close combination of drama and comedy, and this was farce. It was night when a party of Royalists crept down Castle Street to be confronted by Ludlow's men. There were no more than thirty Parliamentarians but the surprise of their counter-attack put the King's men to flight. With the people of Salisbury sitting watching from their windows the Roundheads pursued the Cavaliers up Endless Street which, either belying or confirming its name, was a cul-de-sac. Bottled up, the Royalists realised their only chance was a frontal charge and in a few moments they had their enemies running, like the Keystone Cops, the other way. The spectators must have been like the crowd at the Wimbledon Tennis Championships centuries later, eyes going first one way then the other.

Ludlow's troops had fortified the Cathedral Bell Tower and they hurriedly locked themselves in while Ludlow made himself scarce by crossing the Avon at the Harnham Bridge. It was a flexible battle, to say the least, and Ludlow found his way back to the Bell Tower only to find half his men tucked up in their beds and most of the others absent, having crept away into the night and the countryside.

By now it had dawned on the Royalists that they could win. Their enemies were still in the tower so they kidnapped a blameless working man with a horse and a cart full of glowing charcoal. He was forced to back this smoking load against the main door. In no time the place was busily alight and the Royalists had won. There was a lot of brave shouting but not many fatal casualties, although one was the driver of the horse and charcoal cart. What happened to the horse is not recorded.

At the end of the Civil War the Cathedral had an organist, Giles Tomkins, but no organ. The instrument, which had only just been installed before the hostilities, had been dismantled and secretly stored away. It was a necessary precaution, even for an object as elephantine as a cathedral organ, because Cromwell's men rifled the church and took anything they thought they could sell. All the silver plate disappeared, although some of it was returned by some hangdog soldiers when a Puritan officer had a twinge of conscience. Every ornament, every relic that could be saved was hidden. Some pieces were concealed in ingenious places, and here I have a personal theory. It is unproven and is likely to always remain so: In recent time a treasured 'relic of the Virgin Mary' was discovered in a niche at the very apex of the spire. It was a fragment of cloth, said to have come from a gown or shawl (there are other more exotic descriptions) and was contained in a small metal casket which I have seen in the Cathedral archives. It has always been assumed that this holy item was placed at the top of the spire at the conclusion of its construction in the thirteenth century. But, I think, it may well have been hidden there when Cromwell's soldiers were searching for loot. In those times intrepid choirboys, and some lads from the town, often climbed the steeple – indeed one was known to stand boldly on the topmost crucifix. For a few coins or, in the case of a choirboy, a loaf of bread, the holy icon could have been carried up there and remained safely concealed for centuries. It is only a theory.

The newly-trained and equipped Parliamentary army won the Civil War at the battle of Naseby in 1645. The pikes and swords were put away, the muskets were stacked, the notoriously unreliable artillery was trundled off with relief by its almost suicidal gunners. All the soldiers trudged home.

Christmas was abolished and so were many of the enjoyments of everyday life. The Salisbury Cathedral Close, built with such foresight and precision, began to crumble, roads became overgrown, the graveyard around the church itself began to erupt in a grisly way, rancid streams appeared, a foretaste of the plagues yet to come. Sheep and cattle munched what grass they could find, sometimes they wandered into the Cathedral itself, but there was nothing for them there. All was bare and desolate.

At the end of the Civil War there were only three church figures left, including Giles Tomkins, the organist without an organ; there were remnants of a choir but they had not practised nor learned anything. Wind whistling through the lofty, empty place made the only music. But eventually things changed.

At the end of the sombre Parliamentary days and with the eventual restoration of the monarchy, there were inevitable signs for the better. A new choir began to sing in the still echoing Cathedral. There were seventeen of them and, first things first, they had to be clothed. Each boy's clothing cost, according to the still checkable accounts, £2.18s.4d., but a hat was five shillings extra. Most of these items were made by a lady called Mary Creed who kept a neat record: "For calico to Lyne ye fronts of ye weskett . . . 1s.2d . . . For four dozen and a half of small buttons . . . 1s."

Mary Creed saw a lot of small buttons. Each choirboy's raiment needed 156 of them and the entire choir required the sewing on of 936 buttons. She did every one. It was one woman's contribution to the new dawn in Salisbury and in Britain.

It was a hot day of heavy cloud; the trees around the Cathedral and its Close were listless, dark, and at the gate of what has always been called The Wardrobe, a flag scarcely stirred.

It was at half-mast.

These days The Wardrobe is the museum of the reformed British regiment The Rifles, drawn from the men of Berkshire and Wiltshire. On the previous day, two of the soldiers had been killed in Afghanistan.

Here it was, set and peaceful, the old, steep-roofed building, the umbrellas of the lunch restaurant spread, people drinking wine, the waiters moving smoothly. They used to have a pair of old green field-guns here – pointing towards the gate but they have now been removed to the back of the premises and their useless aim is over the Avon. Why they were moved no one could tell me; perhaps it was to accommodate more parked cars, or because they looked too threatening. Military displays today must be entertaining, like children climbing across the tanks ('Tonnes of Fun') at neighbouring Bovington.

~✺~

How long the building in the corner of The Close has been called 'The Wardrobe' no one seems to know. There is a written margin note on a document dated 1543 "now is called the Wardrobe".

Remarkably, the same family lived in the house from 1659 until 1824, the Coles – four successively (and confusingly) Christian-named William. The last lease-holder was Jane Medlycott, who was also a Coles.

In 1831 the lease was advertised including a description of "a cloistered entrance, a spacious hall with handsome oak staircase, a corridor with secondary staircase, an antique breakfast room, a fine dining room with enriched ceiling and polished floor, a billiard room or library (unfinished) a superb drawing room communicating with a terrace; 8 bedrooms, gallery, butler's pantry and other domestic offices, cellars, w.c., back stairs etc . . . the house has been recently repaired and beautified, at an immense expense, and presents one of the purest specimens of Old English Architecture." It was bought by a Dr. John Grove.

The Wardrobe finally became an adjunct to The Diocesan Training College for School Mistresses – and it may have been from here that Thomas Hardy's sister had a watery encounter in the River Avon.

~✺~

For all their true tales of derring-do and real courage, I always find military museums are sad places. For all the medals and the maps and right back to the muskets, I seem to see the unseen lists of casualties. And they are unending; still going on as I stood there that close afternoon.

Of course I find them interesting. I have written enough about military times to lean forward to read how the regimental drums had to be left behind at Dunkirk.

There are many stories about Dunkirk and one of the best may have come from the soldier who saw those drums abandoned on the beach amid the mayhem that was the evacuation of a whole British army.

This Tommy (as the everyday soldier was called in those days) had walked – not marched; he was alone and tired and from choice you never march alone – the best part of forty miles to the Dunkirk evacuation beach. It was hot and Frenchmen, who might have asked where he thought he was going, would not even give him a cup of water. Bit by bit he abandoned his equipment, although he kept his rifle and at last he arrived at the huge open beach with thousands of troops being taken off under shelling and German dive-bombing. To his astonishment he saw a ferry boat tied up to the jetty, rocking with the explosions, but otherwise intact. He managed to get aboard. The top deck was crammed with exhausted evacuating soldiers, the second deck was a crammed makeshift hospital and operating theatre, but the lower deck was like a miracle – a cool saloon with a white coated steward polishing glasses behind a bar.

Parched as he was the Tommy approached the bar. He could scarcely get the words out from his lips. "Could I have a beer, please." The boat rocked as another shell landed nearby.

"Sorry, soldier." said the steward. "Customs regulations say that we can't serve anything alcoholic until we are outside territorial waters."

⁓

The museum has a scene in the Victorian Sudan when the British first realised that a red uniform made you an easy target; there are muskets and bayonets longer than any man who ever had to use them; there is a battle scene where a realistic hand is reaching out from the mud of Flanders in the First World War – as hopelessly now as it was then.

The cheerfulness breaks through the shadows of the room when old comrades meet there, either by design or accident.

"Do you remember Sergeant Jones of the Orderly Room, A Company."

"Old Josser Jones! I'll say. He stuck in that chair for years. Never saw a day's active service."

They have ghost-watching nights in the museum. I have a problem with this. If the watchers – who pay well for their thrills, real or imagined – are listening for signs of the oldest inhabitants of The Wardrobe, the original clerics, or one of the many William Coles, then that is fun ghost hunting. But if they hope to hear the dead voices of the many dead soldiers remembered there, that is something else.

The half-mast flag at the gate speaks enough for those.

CHAPTER 14

A Ghost at Home

U NTIL A WELL-REMEMBERED AUTUMN evening I had never
entered The Close at Salisbury. I had seen the spire, of
course, it was difficult not to, but I had never been through
the big gates. Then with our gentlemanly but unashamedly
eager estate agent, we drove under the North arch and into
one of England's most calm and lovely places. There were
few people about; the green meadow skirting the Cathedral
was crossed with the shadows of trees, arranged all around
were the fine houses, every one different but all somehow the
same. Anyone who had lived there in the past two centuries
would have had no difficulty in finding their way home.
The Walton Canonry was a classic Georgian oblong, red
brick with three floors of aloof windows, each one looking as
if it could raise an eyebrow, and sometimes did. There was an

upmost parapet (so insecure you could move it with one hand) and hidden behind it the roof, a system of small roofs, in fact, making it look from above oddly like an elevated poultry farm. That evening, the large but delicate drawing room and what became my book-cased study were splashed with the sun setting across the river at the foot of the garden. An Oriental man once came to test the *feng shui* of the panelled study for a newspaper article. He said it was full of old vibes, most of them good, but that my Victorian desk was facing the wrong way. It looked *into* the room which meant that the benign influence of the water, the Avon, was at my back – the wrong way around. I had forgotten to tell the seer that when I was working I sat on the opposite side of the big desk on a chair with a cushion that brought me on a level with my word processor (I am sitting at the same desk on the same chair, but in a different house, writing this on the same keyboard). In this position at the Walton Canonry I was actually facing the fortunate influences from the river. I telephoned the Eastern prophet with this news and he said: "Ah so. Good luck." and put the phone down.

In the garden was a brick-built outhouse known officially as The Bishop's Privy. I used to think that this must be one of the few lavatories covered by a preservation order until I discovered that they were numerous in The Close. The clergy were proud of their privies and showed them off to visitors. Indeed, there was a lot of kudos in the plumbing arrangements; Canon Colcell, who lived in the North Canonry in the 16th century, even had a steam bath installed. It was a monstrous contraption of gleaming pipes and gushing faucets located at the centre of a series of rooms with mysterious doors, designed to preserve the owner's modesty. People used to travel across the country to see this steam bath; it was like the wonder of that world. Whether anyone else was permitted to use it is not on record but as Canon Colcell went around his daily business in The Close people (some unbathed for years) used to waylay him simply to study the pinkness of his skin.

Sometimes, on bright nights, I would look from the bedroom down onto the garden and imagine I could make out an ecclesiastical shade outside the door of the Bishop's Privy. It may have been a moon-trick through the trees. It was hard to imagine with such a commodious house that anyone, even in those former times, would need to find relief in the garden. We used it to shelter the lawnmower.

There was, however, a ghost with more provenance. Robert Key, for years the breezy and popular Member of Parliament for Salisbury, was born in the house (his father was a Bishop) and he recalls: "When I was a small boy my mother would put me to bed and a few minutes later I was convinced she would come into the room and tuck me up for the night. It was a long time until I realised she did nothing of the sort; all that was there was a ghostly hand!" Members of Parliament, even Mr. Key, are of course known for adding entertainment to the truth and we took little notice of this until Matthew, our son, then in his early teens, came to our room at two in the morning and asked, pale-faced, who had been pushing and pulling at his bedclothes.

Over the garden wall was Myles Place, a tall house described by Sir Nikolaus Pevsner as "the finest house in the Cathedral Close". Next to the Cathedral it was arguably the tallest building. Myles Place had been built, or more probably re-built, in the early seventeen hundreds when Salisbury Close was reforming so elegantly around its green and deeply buried churchyard. It was constructed at the same time as our house and probably had the same designer. He must have been a busy man because he cleverly took the outline of the front of The Walton Canonry and built it onto the rear of the house next door. It took a century or more before anyone seemingly noticed. The Myles Place roof was a good watchtower. The extra storey provided a platform from which you could peer far off into the next county, Hampshire, and, more usefully, observe the delicate intricacies, and any loose tiles, within the parapet of our roof next door. We had been required by English Heritage (while keeping its cheque book irrevocably shut) to take this ancient roof apart, number each piece, and put it back together again. The chimneys also had to be rebuilt brick-by-brick. When everything was evening quiet we would see the Cathedral architect, sly as a burglar, climb the scaffolding with a magnet to ensure, we were told, that we were using the authentic nails in the reconstruction. The roof of Myles Place next door was a good vantage point to observe any ancient bits falling out. But there were other things to see from there; a sky-full of bleating geese in autumn. They would swoop, in formation, by the dozen, swerving adroitly around the

Cathedral spire and go headlong for the deep green reeded fields around the water-meadows beyond the Avon.

In the dog-end months of the year, almost every day, we had the delight of half a dozen skies spread with geese, duck or swans. The swans came over on creaking wings, but otherwise silent as ghosts, a contrast to the bedlam of the other birds. The angular swans performed their synchronised manoeuvres with magnificent assurance, never seeming to get a degree wrong in their navigation. It was, therefore, a strange shock to me only a few weeks before writing this to witness one which had got its radar spectacularly awry. It was Sunday afternoon and I was crossing the Harnham Bridge, walking away from my present house, when I heard the swan's wings beating behind me. Then it honked with alarm ("Oh, no!") and, zooming over one parapet of the bridge, crashed full-on into the wall on the opposite side. I was astonished at the impact, (but I bet scarcely more than the swan) although it must have been braking. The collision had a dull, soft thud as though a stuffed mattress had been thrown against the wall. I do not know who recovered first, me or the swan. There was nobody else around (when I told people later it was surprising how many of them just laughed) and I stood, twenty feet away to see what would happen next. Do you go to the aid of a crashed swan? Prudently not.

The swan did not need assistance. It sat up and rubbed its head with its foot; it shook its feathers and took what appeared to be a long accusing look at the bridge ("Where did that come from?") then it wandered groggily into the centre of the road and sat there apparently looking for more trouble. There was little Sunday afternoon traffic but I had to control it around the swan. One driver leaned out and asked: "Is it yours?"

The bird eventually wandered off and when I returned half an hour later was sitting safely by the river in the garden of the St. Nicholas Hospital almshouse where it had been led by the resourceful Warden, the Reverend Jeremy Ames. His wife was at the door with a telephone and they had to rush off to a dangerously ill person. Both the sick person and the swan apparently recovered.

Every morning a bell, tiny and tinny, rings at 9.30 from the St. Nicholas almshouse across the road. It has been doing so for more than three hundred years to call the residents to prayer. They have to go. It is one of the conditions of living in what Jeremy Ames calls "rather posh" accommodation. They go into the delicate chapel for a few minutes and the rest of the day is their own to enjoy in the fine house beside the bending river.

On the same afternoon, after he had dealt with the crashed swan, Jeremy showed me the 1623 chapel bell. It sits in a niche at the side of the stone courtyard of St. Nicholas. It seems its hammer has been striking in the same place for so many years that the metal is almost worn away, a scar runs down the side of the bell. "Looks as if we'll have to move it around a bit before too long." says the man whose official title is The Reverend Master.

He is broad and benign and not much seems to worry

him. You get the impression that his good-natured wife, Angela, does a lot of the everyday worrying for him. He got Christianity early in life but is not strong on ritual. He was once a Royal Navy Chaplain and was seconded for two years with the U.S. Fleet at San Diego, California.,

Trollope published his novel 'The Warden' in the 1850s, set so everyone but Trollope said, at the St. Nicholas almshouse. It caused a bit of a scandal with its depiction of church shenanigans. Jeremy Ames has heard it all but he's not concerned. In real history the almshouse has had enough trouble. Bishop Beauchamp, in the Fifteenth Century, (St. Nicholas itself dates from before the laying of the Cathedral's foundation stones) was concerned with the loose situation at the establishment. Both sexes were accommodated and the bishop had to spell out firm rules: "Brothers and sisters must not behave in a suspicious manner, either in their own rooms or in hidden places."

In early times when there was no bridge across the Avon at Harnham, only a ford, a traveller who used the St. Nicholas accommodation invariably arrived with wet feet. Today, the guests live in something like genteel comfort. Their rooms look out over some of the most placid scenery in Wiltshire and they have a private car park. A greenhouse is also available.

Jeremy Ames is a man of many talents, from handling dis-orientated swans to cooking a classic lunch. Once, during a sombre conversation about mortality, I asked him (since he's years younger than me) if he would conduct my burial service. "All right," he said as if I'd asked to borrow a fiver. "I'll do it." He became stern, *"But not yet."*

Some years before we originally arrived in The Close the historical writer Sir Arthur Bryant had lived at Myles Place. Only a comparatively short time after his death he appears to have disappeared from the modern record books. It is as though he had never written a word. This may, or may not, have something to do with what a selection of people today would call "Jingoism". He was a full-on patriotic Englishman whose books are full of derring-do by the stalwart sons of the British Empire.

Living as he was in the tower of Myles Place, even as the tide of Britishness and patriotism was ebbing, he would, I imagine, have flown a union jack from a flagpole in his garden if the Dean and Chapter had permitted it. They did not. A later occupant of Myles Place, Mr. Roger Croft, actually hoisted a flag by his front gate and was ordered to take it down. The builders working on our heavy alterations were likewise ordered to remove their trade sign. It seemed that the only resident of The Close who could hang out decorations with impunity was Sir Edward Heath who, each Christmas, suspended a couple of hundred twinkling Chinese lights over his front garden. They were a gift from the people of Beijing with whom he was on good terms. (He brought a giant panda to England.) If somebody had suggested he should take his department store illuminations down he probably could have closed his large front door on them. But nobody did.

When the Falklands War began the Daily Express judged that Sir Arthur Bryant possessed the right patriotic passion to quote Britain's case in print and sent Peter Grosvenor, its literary editor, down to Salisbury to write what Sir Arthur had to say. "I thought I would have to re-hash whatever he came out with." remembered Mr. Grosvenor. "But nothing like it. I put the tape recorder in front of him and, with hardly a pause, he dictated a two thousand word article. I was impressed."

There are people living in Salisbury now who remember how shocked they were at a famous dinner party at Myles Place when Sir Arthur, who was over ninety, proclaimed in a pleasant way that he had called them together to announce his engagement to a local young girl who he then brought to the table "'ello," she said shyly and bravely. The astonishment was complete. Anyway, the marriage never took place.

When we moved in next door, Myles Place was the heavily furnished home of Sir Philip Shelbourne who lived there surrounded by great chairs, cupboards and pictures, in the company of a small mongrel dog called, I think, Shelly after the oil company of which Sir Philip had been a director. He was many times a millionaire, a kind man who in his later life rarely went out but looked at the world from his huge windows.

Soon after we arrived he invited us for a drink and we sat in his library trying to take our eyes from the biggest, most beautiful bookcase we had ever seen. After his death it fetched a record price at the auction held in a marquee in the field across the road – almost a quarter of a million pounds.

Most of his fortune went to a donkey sanctuary in the Middle East. I do not remember seeing him very much. He came to our house to a party with two men carrying his wheeled chair like a sedan up the front stone steps. Then, one morning after we returned from a foreign trip, we saw his coffin being carried to the Cathedral. He died as he had lived; privately.

Some months later I was being driven from London when the young man at the wheel said: "I remember bringing Sir Philip Shelbourne down to Salisbury once. Did you know him?"

"He was my neighbour," I said.

"He was a good man. I told him I was going for a job and he bought me a new suit."

"Did you get the job?" I asked.

"No, I didn't. But I've still got the suit."

The auction drew buyers from every part of the world. The Close had never seen such an influx of overseas people since the last Lambeth Conference. The conference always meant that, at some point, The Close was buzzing with bishops from all parts of the world, getting their teeth seen to and having medical problems investigated. It was a busy time for Salisbury dentists and doctors. Who paid I don't know. I didn't think it was the bishops.

The marquee for the Myles Place auction was erected in the cricket field across the road, right on the boundary, and the proceedings lasted three days. We resisted the temptation to open the flap and go in. Both of us are notoriously easy touches when treasures beyond our reach are being auctioned. But on the final afternoon Diana went in and out of desperation bought the last item on the catalogue which had listed hundreds of lots. It was a bright primitive native painting from Haiti. We've still got it somewhere. She paid three pounds for it and, some time later, we were in the Dominican Republic which is joined to Haiti on the Caribbean island of Hispaniola. There were shops festooned with similar paintings from across the border. She had not overpaid. Three pounds was about the going price.

Canon Isaac Walton, who had built our house in about 1720, never lived in it. He was the son of the famous Isaak Walton, but, for some reason had changed the 'k' at the end of his Christian name to a 'c'. It was a pleasant thought to picture the man who wrote 'The Compleat Angler' sitting at the bottom of the garden studying the fish lying below the bank, but unfortunately an anachronism. He also wrote the biography of George Herbert, the amazing man who was vicar of Bemerton, just outside Salisbury. Belatedly the figure of George Herbert has been placed among the ancient saints and historic clerics who decorate the West front of the Cathedral. And it is not out of place.

Herbert sounds suspiciously like the best man who ever lived and Walton was an admiring biographer:

"In Salisbury he saw a poor man with a poorer horse that was fallen under its load. They were both in distress and needed present help which Mr. Herbert, perceiving, put off his Canonical Coat and helped the poor man to unload, and after, to load his horse. The poor man blest him for it: and he blest the poor man and was so like the good Samaritan, that he gave him money to refresh both himself and his horse."

The vicar of Bemerton then went to a musical meeting of friends who could not believe the uncouth state he was in. He was always so 'trim and clean' and they upbraided him for bothering to help someone so "soyled and decomposed". He more or less told them it was his business, not theirs, and brushed himself down with the words "Now, let's tune our instruments."

"His chiefest recreation was musick." Relates Isaac Walton. "In which heavenly Art he was a most excellent Master and did himself compose many divine Hymns and Anthems which he set and sung to his Lute or Viol."

Twice a week this good man would go to the Cathedral to listen to music which he described as his Heaven on Earth. He still found time to administer his parish and take part in a huge range of activities – including righting fallen horses.

Apparently in his plans to build The Walton Canonry Isaac Walton, the son, was frustrated in his intention to demolish the remnants of a former house on the site by a certain Mrs. Hedges, who lived in part of a wing and who stoically refused to be demolished. She has been described as a witch and a sorceress but she was probably just an old woman who wanted to stay in her home. Inevitably she lost her fight and a convenient fire helped to erase the old house. Canon Walton could go ahead.

Having approved the plans Isaac Walton took off to London where he promptly died of cholera. Never upset a witch.

The new house became the property of Francis Eyre whose coat of arms still crowns the massive front door – not just his, but also those of his wife, Anne: "On a chevron three quatrefoils" impaling "a chevron between three lozenges". The first time I walked below them as owner of The Walton Canonry I gave them a diffident, but probably slightly smug nod. At that time Eyre Methuen were my publishers. So I felt there was a bond.

⚬⚮⚬

Just before the outbreak of the Second World War, the young and famous artist Rex Whistler came to live at The Walton Canonry. Various members of his family lived there also during this time including his brother, the fine glass engraver Laurence Whistler. A few months after we had moved in Laurence's son Simon came to the house and in the panelled dining room gave a lecture on glass engraving to about fifty people from The Close. Simon said it was the first time he had been in the house, as far as he could recall, although he understood he had been conceived in the front bedroom.

The family was not connected to the American painter James McNeill Whistler who found fame by painting a pensive study of his mother.

Rex Whistler painted small and he painted huge. In the Museum at The Kings House in The Close, is a collection of neat and engaging studies, mostly of the house and placid garden of his friend Edith Olivier who lived just outside Salisbury. As far as I know he never painted The Walton Canonry nor left any trace of his work there. We looked.

His large work is truly gigantic: the great mural at Plas Newydd in Anglesey, North Wales, and the long-distance landscape – the *trompe l'oeil* – he painted around the wall of what is now the restaurant of the Tate Gallery, the old one, in London. This latter mural stretches around the sides of the expansive room. I have often thought what a pleasure and diversion it would be to sit at a lunch table alone and study the figures and the mysterious background an inch at a time. You would then switch to the other side of the room, for your pudding course, and occupy yourself with the next few miles of scene. It would take three hours at a minimum so it might be as well to order a brandy.

Paths lead secretly into folding hills, people move slyly, and animals pause about their grazing; there are half-hidden houses and glimpses of shadowy water. Every inch has a question, a clue or an answer, an invitation to continue a mythical journey from soup to cheese and biscuits.

There are touches of Rex Whistler's work in many places. To say he became engrossed in the smallest of details in a huge canvas goes without saying. So it must have been a rude interruption on the morning of Sunday, September 3rd 1939, when he was deep in a detail of a decoration at Mottisfont Abbey, not far from Salisbury, and someone came in and told him that Britain and Germany were at war. He is said to have muttered an expletive and, to emphasise it, worked it into the space he was painting. People still try to spot it today – a deeply felt curse from more than half a century ago. He was never to see the end of the war. He enlisted in The Welsh Guards and was killed a few weeks after D-Day in 1944 near Caen in Normandy. Something jammed in the track of his tank and, disregarding the basic orders ("Never leave your tank") and his own safety, he climbed out to free the obstacle. A German mortar shell exploded nearby killing him.

⌇

Salisbury Cathedral is overloaded with memorials to importantly dead people. They vary from the ponderous to those verging on the light-hearted, from the dusty and ornate to the simplest slab; some of the marble figures stare out, lost for words, apparently not sure what they are doing there.

The memorial to Rex Whistler is, without argument, the most serene in the huge place. And it is never still. You can find it on the wall of the Morning Chapel, hardly bigger than the face of a grandfather clock, a solid but delicate glass prism, the work, of course, of Laurence Whistler. As it slowly revolves it shows the spired Cathedral and – up in the celestial clouds – two images of The Walton Canonry. It is, literally, wonderfully moving.

CHAPTER 15

On the Wild Side

A NOVEMBER MORNING; I LEFT the kitchen door as a man on Radio Four was saying emphatically: "November is the dreariest month of the year" and walked towards the river. It looked like he was right; the water like lead, the landscape flat but just protruding from its mist; the sky on the verge of tears. Then there came a great clamour from beyond the view and, in their own beautiful time, came a chevron of geese, stretching from horizon to horizon, the most I had ever seen. They came on necks stretched towards their distant quest. There was no time to count them. I could only stand entranced.

From the green river banks of all the houses on that side of The Close there is a landscape (sometimes a waterscape) even older, less changed than that of The Close itself – the

Harnham Watermeadows. Winter, like some old, grey, grumbling friend, was coming on that day. The meadows were sage, lying low, mist caught in bushes. Miles away it seemed, although it was not that far, was the silhouette of Harnham Mill, tall at one end, lower at the other, the shape of a ship – a container ship. Nothing moved; I was aware of that deep pleasure of open air silence.

Living in a place like that you came across many curious things.

We had an ornamental pond on one side of the garden, near the Bishop's Privy, the home of some tubular coloured fish which we had brought from our previous house. My dog used to spend somnolent summer afternoons flat on his stomach just staring at their languid inactivity, perhaps envious of their life. One morning from the bathroom above I saw a kingfisher alight on the head of the stone nymph figure standing in the middle of the pond. I stood admiring his colours and suddenly I realised he was doing the same to the fish. They saw him too and panicked, diving to the deepest part of the pond except one, the senior fish, who was bigger than the bird and knew it. When he had wriggled into range he dipped his orange tail and sent a dollop of water with amazing accuracy into the kingfisher's face. I had never seen a shocked kingfisher before. It jumped and fluttered but then settled on its position again, just in time to receive another soaking from the resourceful carp. That was enough; no breakfast was worth that. He flew away wet and still hungry.

There was a place where, if you sat still long enough, on

a summer night you would hear the warm plop of a water vole as it slid into the river; one morning we awoke to see a black swan had appeared. It was surrounded by our local swans viewing it with the sort of suspicion you might experience on realising a relative from Western Australia had turned up unannounced and you had no idea how long he intended staying.

There is another story, about a sheep and a rabbit which nobody believes except that Matthew, my son, a teenager at the time, saw it with me. We were sitting, each philosophically downing a pint on the waterside lawn of The Rose and Crown, one June evening. It was so quiet you could hear us slurp. Across the river in the short field at the end of the water-meadows, some of Mr. Beeton's Soay sheep were munching. They are a prehistoric breed and they originally lived on the far-out islands of St. Kilda off the Hebrides, although these came from Salisbury Plain. These sheep's forebears may have been around for eons but I wager none has ever had a fight with a rabbit – and lost. The bone of contention (if it could be termed that) was a tuft of thick grass. Matthew and I could see this was a special tuft. The sheep was already nosing it when the bulky rabbit appeared. They faced each other, both took a chew at the stuff and then the rabbit retreated several paces before launching himself, like a fat rocket, at the sheep, hitting him squarely on the nose. The sheep clearly did not know what to do. It stood staring. The rabbit backed off again and flung itself through the air, once more butting the sheep on the nose. That was it. The sheep retired, the rabbit munched the grass.

⌒∾⌒

Mr. Beeton, who owned the Soay sheep (and, I suppose, the rabbit since it was in his field) was a man of many parts. He ran a little garage business just outside The Close. He was a chorister and he sometimes concealed a small engine part below his cassock and took it out and cleaned it during a long and possibly dull Cathedral sermon.

⌒∾⌒

The water meadows are really an island – in shape not unlike a miniature Isle of Wight – almost a hundred acres squeezed between the muscular rush of two rivers, the Avon and the Nadder. Every winter the land was 'drowned', the sluices opened making the meadows a lake. When spring dawned it produced a thick crop of fine grazing much appreciated by the black-faced Salisbury sheep. In the heyday of the horse, cartloads of it were also carried into Salisbury as feed. The drowning is still accomplished to a limited degree and at the last reckoning 260 sheep were feeding, with 175 lambs and one llama. Sadly the llama has recently died; he looked after the sheep like a big brother. A replacement has just been found.

There are tracks and trails across the meadows and volunteers, devoted and often soaked to the knees, keep up repairs and some sort of order to the wilderness. But the fact that there is a magic about the low landscape, with its scenery across the reeds and water to yet another aspect of the Cathedral, does not seem to enter the consciousness of some people; huge bags of litter are collected. But these wild places are not easy to order; nature has a mind of her own. In Victorian days there was a regular panic whenever Henry Fawcett, Britain's Post Master General, and a local resident, decided to take a walk across the meadows. Paths had to be clear and bridges in good condition because Mr. Fawcett, despite being responsible for several million letter deliveries every day, was blind.

Some people seek out a hidden cranny, even in the sparse land and observe the bird life. Apart from the water fowl, who noisily inhabit the whole region, the watchers' patience has been rewarded in recent times by the appearance of the little egret, the great spotted woodpecker and the kestrel among dozens. The grey heron is easily detected because he does not shift, merely stares into the water with the deep interest of a bingo player. The Cathedral spire falcon is only recorded by the remains of his meals.

About six miles away is a colony of buzzards. I have seen their raucous family gatherings in winter-bare trees and in summer enjoyed their sky-high flights, mewing like cats. They are a pleasure for the bird-watchers but not for the other birds. When they decide to circle the spire of the Cathedral they are violently mobbed by crows, encouraged by smaller birds egging them on. They soon give up and go home.

In France, particularly among the monks and agrarian priests, floating or drowning the land was an annual event. The water was never wasted. On its flowing journey from the fields to the abbey lavatories it was siphoned off for cooking, cleaning and brewing beer. The French peasants also recruited it as a weapon in their unending war in the fields against what they called the "moldye-warpes". Moles are always a menace.

Further west from Salisbury, in Dorset around the hamlets of the Piddle Valley, Piddlehinton and Affpuddle there were water meadows. I remember doing some army training down there; our boots were never dry.

At the height of summer the Harnham meadows are vibrating with life; insects, birds and water creatures, including children who wade waist-deep in the rushing rivers. There are few trees but the bushes and hedges are bursting and the sky is wide and blue. But I always think that the meadows are at their best when there is a sense of sadness about them. Some people, and I am occasionally among them, find an enjoyment in melancholy places, grey and flat landscapes, wind scraping through low branches, dark ruffled water. It was the American, Robert Frost, who wrote:

> *"My Sorrow, when she's here with me,*
> *Thinks these dank days of autumn rain*
> *Are beautiful as days can be."*

These days you take a road that narrows to an old path between some suburban Salisbury houses to find yourself beside the Harnham Mill and its streams. The mill wheel has long gone and no one apparently bothered to record its passing. But from the fifteenth century it revolved uncomplainingly to give power to a variety of industry – breaking up wool, fulling as it was called, papermaking when paper was the new miracle material. Fulling required people to stand for hours in tubs stamping out the raw wool, a monotonous task that must have been hard on the feet.

There are legends that, long before this, the mill was used as accommodation for the nuns of Wilton Abbey while their abbey was "sweetened", its windows and doors thrown open and God's air admitted. Long after that, the mill reversed its role, it became a tallow factory –giving out odour that stopped horses in their tracks. Go there today and you can have a decent pint of beer and a jacket potato with a range of fillings. The walls, within and without, give signs of the age of the place.

Outside was a mud-coated land-rover with three cheerful and equally daubed men resting, each enjoying a pint, at their feet were spread a clutch of shot waterfowl and a four foot dead hare.

"Good bag," I mentioned.

The leading man looked up amiably. "Proper job," he said without a flicker. "Bought 'um in Salisbury Market 'smornin'."

But it is a place shadowed by a tragedy. Alongside the dark, thick water, is a seat with a plaque, recently put there to commemorate an act of bravery by a twenty year old woman, a student at the Sarum St. Michael College in The Close. Susan Harris was about to be married. On this March day in

1966 she lost her life trying to save a nine year old boy who had fallen in the cold water. She is buried beside the Cornish church at Rame, where she was to have been wed. Her family carried the biggest stone they could find on the beach and used it to mark her grave. There is a memorial window to her in Salisbury Cathedral. Her fiancé from those days, Victor Flute, and his wife Helen, who had been Susan's closest friend from the college, came to the unveiling of the seat many years after the tragedy. Two Salisbury men, one the boy who had fallen in the river and the other who also attempted to rescue him, were also there.

Victor and Helen, brought strangely together by the tragedy, have grandchildren and live in Suffolk. So there is a happy ending.

CHAPTER 16

Salisbury Docks

FIVE RIVERS COME TOGETHER AT Salisbury. The Avon, like a sinewy forearm, goes determinedly to enter the English Channel at Christchurch. If that is the arm, Salisbury City is the hand and the fingers are four lesser rivers. The thumb is missing.

If plans and dreams and money had worked out there could also have been a canal stretching straight from the smooth green banks of The Cathedral Close, mixing with the river with an elbow to the east and on to Southampton. For the best part of two hundred years watermen and businessmen sniffed around the plans, models were modelled and stretches have been excavated and the useless work the navvies did can still be witnessed at Britford and other places. Business meetings were regularly called and just as regularly the cash ran out.

Two men who had a seventeenth century dream that the canal would one day link the city with the sea were John Taylor who called himself 'The Water Poet' and John Ivie, a brave and popular mayor of Salisbury. Taylor, in 1623, attempted to demonstrate the possibilities by single-handedly rowing a wherry, a large but lightly floating barge, from London to Christchurch and then on to Salisbury. He wrote an account of his voyage, quite a lot of it by inland water: 'Discovery by Sea with a Wherry from London to Salisbury'. Swans, apparently overcome with curiosity, escorted him in flocks along the river part of his exploration. At Ringwood welcoming trumpets were sounded and Lord Dundalk opened his cellars and his wallet. But Taylor sailed up the Avon to Salisbury at night and few noticed he had arrived. He stayed at The King's Head but the moment of triumph had gone; there was no thanksgiving in the Cathedral which, had matters progressed, would have faced a busy waterfront and busy future. John Ivie was the mayor and hero of the citizens for his solo bravery during The Plague (he paid the 'bring out your dead' men four shillings a week, provided extra Bibles and fired a musket over their heads when they went on strike). Today, Ivy street is named after him.

But the two men got nowhere with their vision of a canal. Taylor, however, was given the money to buy a new wherry by Lord Dundalk – to replace his "tattered, wind-shaken and weather-beaten boat".

Enthusiasm in seventeenth century Salisbury was never overwhelming and although there were existing canals in the region, at Bristol, Devizes and at nearby Andover, few people thought a waterway from The Cathedral Close to the Southampton dockyards would work. They could hear the toot of the first railway train. The matter was finally laid to rest when a locomotive steamed into Salisbury. The Avon was left to the fish and fishermen and as the apt foreground to the climbing spire, which it remains today.

Now that the wool and cloth industry diminished after making the city and the countryside prosperous (London prostitutes proudly wore scarves of "Salisbury cloth and colours") and the watermills slowed, the rivers sank once again into the landscape.

It had been a good try by some enthusiasts. After all, some of the Portland stone used by the early Cathedral masons was surely floated up-river and two fully laden barges of general cargo were towed as far as the Harnham Bridge in 1684 just to show it could be done. If it had been done then, what is today a hamlet of pretty houses – including my own – built around the De Vaux settlement immediately outside the Harnham Gate might have been transformed into a place of warehouses, customs posts, cranes and taverns. We could have been Salisbury Docks.

The slim rivers that descend to the Avon at Salisbury bubble and slip from low hills. Villages up there were built by the Saxons and it is not difficult to find some of the nuggets of history. The aristocracy lived in fine places but the aristocrats left to go off to strange lands to fight. There is a Crusades-age church up there with the tomb of a local knight who killed seventeen Saracens in a single encounter and then escaped by swimming the Nile. A gentler Wiltshire river flows nearby and carved at the knight's feet is not the usual faithful dog but, to commemorate his adventure, an otter.

These little rivers are fed by even smaller ones, the winter-bournes, like the shy River Rill, which flow only until April and then after September – Winterbourne Zelston, Winterbourne Gunner, Winterbourne Dauntsey and so on. There are no fewer than sixteen Winterbournes in Wiltshire and Dorset. In the summertime they are stone dry, the home of marsh marigolds and frogs. These slender tributaries avoided the old castle and cathedral on its blank mound at Old Sarum. The lack of water was one of the reasons the original monks could not leave quickly enough. With the spiteful soldiers locking the only well the brothers who had gone there to praise God in comfort found themselves humping buckets and goatskins of water up the steep climb.

Around the new Cathedral and its growing town water flowed copiously, perhaps too much so. As the Salisbury streets were built so the shabby channels were dug along them. Some of today's streets turn corners simply to follow the flow of the streams. Every sort of rubbish, and worse, went into the waterways and continued to do so for years.

The inhabitants could not comprehend why two hundred of their fellow citizens died in the cholera outbreak in a few summer weeks in 1849. Thirteen hundred new cases were briskly despatched to an isolation hospital – next to a sewage-carrying stream "discoloured and offensive to the smell". Well into the nineteenth century townspeople were blithely emptying their human slops into the waterway and only yards away others were drawing drinking water. One day some men digging believed they had struck a medicinal spring, the water rich and brown, and eagerly sampled it. It was then revealed as a cess pit. Some visitors apparently did not notice. Daniel Defoe wrote with enthusiasm: "The people of Salisbury are gay and rich, and have a flourishing trade; and there is a good deal of good manners and good company among them; I mean among the citizens, beside what is found among the gentlemen." He praised the city's industry and endeavour, but probably did not taste the water.

'The Salisbury Journal', first published in 1715 at three ha'pence, encouraged the picture of a thriving city, despite the drainage. One of the first provincial newspapers to include advertisements, it was moved to proclaim its worth:

> *If any gem'man wants a wife*
> *(A partner, as 'tis term'd, for life)*
> *An advertisement does the thing*
> *And quickly brings the pretty thing.*
> *If you want health, consult our pages,*
> *You shall be well, and live for ages;*
> *Our empirics, to get them bread,*
> *Do every thing – but raise the dead.*
>
> *Lands may be had, if they are wanted,*
> *Annuities of all sorts granted;*
> *Places, preferments, bought and sold;*
> *Houses to purchase, new and old.*
> *Ships, shops, of every shape and form,*
> *Carriages, horses, servants swarm;*

No *matter* whether good or bad,
We tell you where they may be had.
Our services you can't express,
The good *we* do you hardly guess;
There's not a want of human kind,
But we a remedy can find.

CHAPTER 17

By the Water

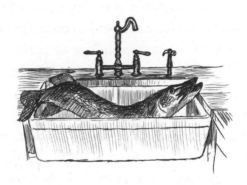

EVERY YEAR THOUSANDS OF CAMERAS are aimed at Salisbury Cathedral: photographs are taken inside and out, up to the top of the spire and down again. There is no niche, nor corbel that has not ended up in someone's album. The grinning stone faces of gargoyles, fulfilling their useful existence as the mouths of roof drains, are taken back to Salisbury, Maryland, USA and many other foreign spots, and shown off to those who have never made the journey.

But one unique image was never, as far as I can discover, captured and kept. On 5th January, 1915, after saturating downpours had continued for days, water rose from the Cathedral floor and lay there like a lake and a mirror. The flat, patterned reflection of the glorious interior roof and walls of the building could be seen cast for the first time and the last. No one seems to have thought to take a picture. You can see the flood level today marked by a brass plaque at the western end of the North Nave aisle. It simply says: "Flood Level – 5th January, 1915".

The actual scene had even more interest. A service was in progress (perhaps the Old Testament reading was about Noah and the Ark) and continued as the water gurgled up through the floor of the nave and around the shins of the congregation. A makeshift pulpit was contrived and the sermon was doggedly preached while the congregation sat with its feet in the rising and freezing flood.

There are conflicting accounts of the arrival at the service of Dr. Bourne, a canon, (one of several known for his eccentricity). Dora Robertson, the wife of the Cathedral School headmaster, wrote that the Canon was confronted by a lake in the Churchyard and imperturbably took off his boots and stockings and rolled up his trousers. Then he balanced on some planks placed over the flood and reached the North door, splashing coldly but it appears happily up the nave to the choir. The second account varies. Salome Pelly, the biblically named daughter of Bishop Wordsworth, relates that her father remembers Canon Bourne taking off more than his shoes and stockings to cross the floodwater to the Cathedral. He looked like "primaeval man" – stark naked.

⟨⟩

Enclosed between low hills and Salisbury Plain, the city and its Cathedral have a variety of damp weather. At one time there was even a special ailment emanating from it called, I think, The Salisbury Fugue. Sufferers coughed in a low register.

At the end of the eighteenth century, Bishop John Douglas made his personal weather notes:

"Salisbury is the sink of Wiltshire places," he wrote. "The Close is the sink of Salisbury and the Bishop's Palace is the sink of the Close."

There were serious floods every few years. In early days the gentry rode into Evensong on horseback and the clergy on mules and donkeys. The saving grace in the town was that the rush of water scoured out the fever-bearing waterways and left them, for a while, clean and wholesome. But before long the drains became blocked again and when summer came Salisbury could be sniffed out by travellers before the spire had come into view.

Almost buried in brambles clogging a copse at the foot of our garden in The Close there were some odd relics, the main one being a big, cogged wheel, rusty and heavy.

Even into the twentieth century, some waterways had continued to flow. (New Canal Street is the most recognisable relic, although the canal has gone). On a nineteen-thirties map I saw a channel marked running from the small lake in the grounds of the Cathedral School – until 1946 the Bishop's Palace - across two roads and a field, sidling by one of our front gates into the garden and then down to the bank of the Avon. The rusty but still sturdy wheel and the rest of the old iron were part of a sluice gate.

Today it is easy to trace this watercourse with the naked eye. It came from the lake, ducked under one narrow road in The Close, then between the cricket field and the rugby pitch on a line clearly to be seen by two lines of pollarded willows. The West Walk has a tunnel-sized bump where the stream progresses into the garden of The Walton Canonry, where it is lost to sight until it reaches the river. These days there is no evidence of any water flowing through it. There was an inlet where the sluice used to be and when we were shoring up the river bank we uncovered a colony of eels. They looked enormous to me, each one as big as an arm, and they appeared affronted that, after probably years, they had been disturbed. Our workmen carried one off; they knew about catching fish. One day I came home to find a full-grown pike in the kitchen sink.

My own tangled efforts at justifying the riparian rights that went with the house were never more than half-hearted despite the lessons of the sage Walter Partridge. My cast of a line seemed unerringly to get caught in branches even when there did not seem to be trees. I wondered sometimes how the trees had sprouted and grown while I was trying to get the hook attached to the line. I tried to tie flies and ended up cursing. Only a solitary fish ever fell to my wiles. I could see it lying fatly under the riverbank, encouragingly idling against the flow of the river. The bait more or less fell into its mouth. With much misgiving I hooked him as gently as I could and brought him to the grass on the bank. There he lay, panting and regarding me hurtfully. I looked at him. It was no good. I took the hook from his mouth and slid him into the river. In ten years living there I never even tried to catch a fish again. I did not like the way they stared.

One winter, looking out from the house towards the Avon, we saw that the river had disappeared below a huge lake that stretched beyond the Water Meadows. It was like peering out into the Atlantic. The flood water was half-way up the long lawn which, fortunately, sloped up towards the house. There were swans enjoying their new roomy world and ducks were floating in our rose beds.

⸻ ⁓ ⸻

There always seemed to be something occurring on the river. On our very first morning in the house, a police helicopter came so low over us that I worried for our expensively replaced roof. It landed on the far bank and there came some urgent activity including a lot of flashing and flapping about with that silver-foil rescue stuff they use. A phalanx of policemen were surrounding a man and trying to keep him upright. We had to wait for that week's 'Salisbury Journal' for the story. The man had ended up in the river the morning after a night's drinking. His rescue and arrest had, however, been hindered by the fact that he had only one arm and, more seriously, only one leg.

Every year men used to float up on flat boats to drag the summer-grown weed from the surface but, oddly, these were almost the only boats we saw in ten years on the Avon. A family once paddled upstream in an Indian canoe but found it too arduous against the stream and turned around and went back the easier way.

Two brave giggling girls one day swirled by languorously lying in rubber inner-tubes and on another morning two lads appeared aboard a home-made raft, floating on oil drums and with a wobbling mast. They were like Tom Sawyer and

Huckleberry Finn. They had put together the contraption and were paddling using two old cricket bats on the first stage of a journey of discovery and exploration. They said they had pickle sandwiches and two bottle of Fanta. They were not sure where they would end up. "Ringwood," said one modestly. "France," said the other. They did not get as far as even Ringwood. Late in the same afternoon I saw them laboriously plying their cricket bats against the current. It took them twenty minutes to cover the width of the garden.

"Didn't get to France then?" I said

"The fishing bloke sent us back," said one.

"The bailiff," said the other.

They paddled on. I felt it was a shame. Nobody turned Columbus back.

On warm days, or better still warm evenings, we would go down and splash in the river. Swim was scarcely the word because at that season the water was low. It wriggled rather than flowed. We had once, a few years before, had a little wooden house on an island in the Thames and there was plenty of room, and depth, for swimming. We also saw more boats of an evening than we saw in ten years of evenings at Salisbury. Sometimes they were not even the right way up; they were always colliding in Marlow Lock and my basset, Furlong, would filch people's picnics when they were not looking. But that was another, now distant, story.

In the nineteen-twenties the choirboys and the others from the Cathedral School used to swim *en masse* in the Avon. It was not perfect for, as we found years later, the bottom was both stony and squelchy with forests of reeds. The boys must have been glad when a new municipal swimming bath was opened in the town – ingeniously warmed by pipes from the steam laundry next door. The proud, painted sign of the steam laundry is still there.

When we bathed in the Avon the dog would watch respectfully from the bank but more proximate witnesses were the ducks and the white beaked curious coots who would whiz around in circles to see what we were doing, occupying their space.

The schoolboys of the twenties used to scoop up bucketsful of crayfish from the river and take them back for their tea. All we ever found (apart from the colony of eels) were thousands of pieces of blue and white china. With patience you could have assembled a whole dinner service from the shards. The puzzle was how did it all get into the river? Was it thrown in bit by bit when a plate or a bowl was broken or did someone in the nineteenth century fling them there in a fit of pique after a failed dinner party? The odd thing was that the school playing field on the other side of the house was sown with thousands of sea shells. My brother-in-law brought his metal detector and swept the whole of our garden for treasure. No gold or jewels nor even common coins turned up, although I did at a later time find a penny from 1902 in our greenhouse.

In her engaging book Dora Robertson, the headmaster's wife, evokes a summer's day in 1926 when the Cathedral School staged not just a regatta but a carnival on the Avon. A piano was towed downriver on a rickety craft called the

'Ironclad' which had only just discharged its load when it sank never to sail again.

She sets the scene in her book: "The decorated and illuminated boats went down the river to a point opposite Leadenhall. Canon Myers had invited a large number of guests. The seven boats held, respectively, a 'Nigger Wedding', 'The King's Breakfast', 'A Midsummer Night's Dream' . . ."All the boys for whom there was no room in the boats went on foot down The Close as the Lost Boys from Peter Pan. Later with the piano safely landed in the meadow, there was a concert: 'sea shanties' and 'nigger songs' were sung." It was the story of a happy day in an age of innocence. Dora would not have been able to publish it like that today.

River people, those who live by contemplative waters anyway, tend to be contemplative themselves. The Avon is a thoughtful river, broad, pensive; meandering (the very word from the River Meander, slow and sinuous in ancient Anatolia). Much of the Avon, as it wanders from Salisbury, through the green flatlands of lower Hampshire, is inaccessible, there are no roads, not even paths, just ways known to few that lead to its banks.

A big thoughtful man called Aylmer Tryon lived in Kingfisher Mill and had something of the river about him. Nothing appeared to give him a moment's worry and he almost drifted casually into our lives at Salisbury.

It was difficult to be unobtrusive that June day because we had three hundred people for a charity dinner in a huge marquee on our lawn. There was a cricket match with half a dozen England players performing on the school pitch in front of the house. My God, but I enjoyed that day! I captained the team representing The Lord's Taverners and took the greatest catch of my hitherto undistinguished cricket life. Brian Johnston, the legendary "Johnners" of BBC commentary fame, witnessed it and noted (on the first page, mark you) in his famous book 'From the Boundary' "He took a sizzling catch and threw it in the air like a professional". There must have been a thousand spectators (and, truthfully, as the ball sizzled towards me on the boundary, I had a quick worry that we might not be insured for damage to onlookers!)

Anyway, into this summer scene arrived Aylmer Tryon. He did not have a ticket, nor did he pay, but he came to lunch and dinner and charmed everyone. He later invited us to a charity auction at the house of Lord and Lady Tryon – the latter the famous 'Kanga' – given that nickname by Prince Charles. The charity was not for some humanitarian cause but for a new heavy roller for the village cricket pitch.

Later I took Kanga's son to an England — Australia Test Match at the Oval. He was about fourteen and during the tea interval announced that he was off to get the autographs of the Australian Team. I protested that this would be impossible, he would never get near the dressing room, but he came back with every name signed. I had forgotten that his godfather – Prince Charles – at that time owned the ground.

Aylmer Tryon sent me a copy of his beguiling book on fishing 'The Quiet Waters By'. In it he remembers the Old

Mill overlooking the River Avon which used to shake as the corn was ground. Later he realised a dream and bought the Mill and steadied it. *"Now I write in a room with the river flowing beneath, surrounded by birds and animals and indeed fish, all attracted by the food the river provides; flies for the fish, swallows, wagtails and warblers; the little fish for kingfishers and dabchicks, if they survive being pursued relentlessly by the grey herons. The swaying river weeds are the home of shrimps, caddis and larvae, and for my friends the water voles, who sit patiently munching weeds which they often hold in their little paws beneath swaying willow boughs."*

He was a man content.

CHAPTER 18

Constable at Work

ONE MORNING IN EARLY SPRING a large highly patterned man of middle-age trudged along the far bank of the river carrying an easel and a stool. His shirt looked huge, broad red and white, as a banner. He wore bulging jeans and, once he had settled his belongings, placed a Panama hat on his sparse hair. I knew he was American. He looked like Teddy Roosevelt.

"Really nice day," he called.

I agreed it was and watched him set up his easel and paints and a stool so small I thought it would never support him. I went back into the house but when I returned half-an-hour later he was still not settled. He was moving his canvas, a yard this way, a yard that. This time we did not converse. I went away and came back after another hour. He was humped before his canvas, looking, squinting directly across the river towards me, over the edge of the Leadenhall School garden, over some small trees to where the Cathedral spire and a bit of the Cathedral itself was visible around the flank of our house. It was as if the Cathedral was playing a game, peeping at him.

"I just can't get it darned right," the man called across, as though he felt he owed me an explanation. "Maybe it's moved." He regarded whatever he had done on the canvas and stood back. "Ah, hell," he said without vigour. "It's all been done before."

That went without saying. The result ended up gracing the wall of The National Gallery in London – 'Salisbury Cathedral from the River' or 'The Garden at Leydenhall'. John Constable painted it in 1820. My American friend could only have been a few yards from the place where the first sketch was made.

Leadenhall was one of the original Canon's houses in The Close. It was given to Elias de Dereham, the chief builder of the Cathedral. It had a double plot and, uniquely, a lead roof, hence its name. Portions of it remained until 1915 when it was demolished before it fell down of its own accord.

The easy-flowing Avon is in the foreground of the painting and there is a small boat moored by the opposite bank and a group of people sitting by the water. The rest of the painting seems full of summer trees set before a full sky.

Clouds were part of Constable's being. He was a tough-tongued man who stood his ground even against Bishop John Fisher of Salisbury who was his original mentor. Fisher was not one to temper his words either (he once described the Dean of

Winchester as "hobbling along, spouting Greek and spittle"). He did not like Constable's turbulent skies. In the famous painting of the Cathedral from the grounds of the Bishop's Palace, Bishop Fisher and his wife are in the foreground, "I wish to have a more serene sky." He complained: "If Constable would but leave out his black clouds." His nephew, Archdeacon Fisher (also John) Constable's great friend informed the artist: "The bishop likes your picture all but the clouds he says. He likes a clear blue sky." But the artist would not shift. Painting, he said, was another word for feeling. "A landscape painter," he said. "Who does not make his skies a very material part of his composition, neglects to avail himself of one of his greatest aids."

He was not, he said bitterly, a "ladies' and gentlemen's painter." He painted as he saw. The work was hung unaltered in the Victoria and Albert Museum.

Constable, son of a Suffolk miller, knew he was a difficult man. He delivered sarcasm with a soft voice, reserving much of this for his fellow artists. He was said to have warmth and deep feelings but he made unpalatable comments. In a curious way this sharp edge to his judgments was reflected in his writing. The man who attained such glory in his art on canvas could scarcely write. Letters which survive show an extraordinary ignorance about even basic English. Some, seeking an excuse for this carelessness, put it down to the fact that his quills were wearing out.

Spelling was haphazard, he threw capital letters at the

page with abandon, commas and full stops appear at random, and there are meaningless dashes slashed across the text. He has proved a nightmare for his biographers.

He came to Salisbury solely because of his long friendship with Archdeacon John Fisher, the Bishop's nephew. Without that friendship it is doubtful if the famous and glorious paintings of the Cathedral would have been achieved. He did not particularly like the city. "Salisbury has offered some sketches," he wrote offhandedly after his first visit in 1811. "I did not however do so much as I might while I was there. I was not in the humour." He also thought the local weather was "muggy" and the younger Archdeacon loyally agreed: "you are quite correct. Salisbury *is* a nasty, damp, muggy place."

They must have been a strange pair. Constable was well aware of his moods and sarcasms. He spoke of his "vexed career" and had nothing but contempt for many of his contemporaries, artists and others. But John Fisher could only see his bursting talent. He was far from being a rich man but he did all he could to act as a mentor to the raw man from Suffolk.

He encouraged the painter to marry Maria Bicknell (offering to perform the ceremony himself) against the wishes of her parents. After the marriage the couple embarked on a leisurely tour by stage coach which touched south-west England and ended with a few days at Leydenhall (as it was then called). This was the substance of the tradition that Constable spent his honeymoon in Salisbury. However John Fisher, his friend and financial supporter, was anxious for him to return to The Close. Fisher was one of the few men that Constable felt unable to treat with sarcasm. He once wrote to him: "I have no patron but yourself – and you are not the Duke of Devonshire or any other great ass. You are a gentleman and a scholar . . ."

After the younger man's death in 1832 Constable wrote: "We loved each other . . . and his loss makes a sad gap in my life."

It was Fisher who insisted that John and Maria should stay at Leydenhall whenever they pleased. "You shall have a plate of meat set by the side of your easel without you sitting down to dinner: we never see company . . . My wife is quiet and silent and sits and reads without disturbing a soul and Mrs. Constable may follow her example. Of an evening we will sit over an autumnal fireside, read a sensible book, perhaps a Sermon, and after prayers get us to bed at peace with ourselves and all the world."

What is astonishing is that, despite this offer of kindnesses, Constable only visited Salisbury on a meagre handful of occasions over several years, and yet produced nine major paintings and many sketches in pen and pencil and watercolour. From 1811, when he lodged at the Palace with Bishop Fisher, to 1829 after the early death of Maria, and under a deep depression, he stayed at Leydenhall with John Fisher, the archdeacon, on three occasions. The total of the visits to Salisbury is under ten. From these scattered days came the grand views of the Cathedral and its surroundings from every aspect, except the north. There were no grand trees from that view.

J. M.W. Turner was a contemporary of Constable and he turned his massive talents to paintings of the Cathedral from the interior as well as exterior views. His studies of the Chapter House are full of height and smoky hollows. Miniature figures make it appear larger and more mysterious. Today the same splendid building, in use all the time, has little of the remoteness seen by Turner. Although your eyes immediately rise up the octagonal walls it purveys no distant mystery only a sense of comfort and security.

Constable, although he could not deny the other artist's talent, believed Turner was too commercial and took too many money-paying commissions to the detriment of his art; a "ladies' and gentlemen's" painter indeed. One of the outstanding works of Constable's Salisbury collection 'Salisbury Cathedral from the Meadows' would not let him rest. He re-worked it for years, made its sky more black, more turbulent and finally added a vivid rainbow.

The painting was proposed to be his memorial in the National Gallery after his death in March, 1837. It was described in the 'Morning Post' as "Mr. Constable's coarse and vulgar imitation of Mr. Turner's freaks and follies" and was finally rejected.

Today the great John Constable is represented by a gentler, more pastoral work – 'From the River' painted at the bottom of the garden next to ours in Salisbury Close.

CHAPTER 19

Tales of Thomas Hardy

WHERE THERE IS HISTORY SO there is mystery; the longer the history the deeper the mystery. Salisbury has many mysteries, not all of them distant in time. There were two concerning the novelist Thomas Hardy, neither of which has ever been completely explained:

1. Did he "marry" his beautiful cousin Tryphena in a phantom service at midnight in St. Thomas' Church, Salisbury, a few hours before she was to marry another man? Did he and Tryphena have a secret child?

2. What happened to his sister Mary, a student at the Teachers' Training College, in the Kings House in The Close? Somehow Mary ended up in the River Avon and somehow did not drown. Did she fall? Did she jump? Was she pushed?

Hardy was plain "Tom Hardy" before, to the joy of his large working class family, he wrote his famously downcast novels, 'Tess of the D'Urburvilles', 'Far from the Madding Crowd', and notably 'Jude the Obscure'. Then he became Thomas Hardy. Tom was never mentioned again.

The Hardys were rural folk, Dorset jobbing builders. Each was encouraged to better himself, to get rid of the terrible label of "trade-family". Thomas himself was deeply cut when he applied to study at Salisbury with the intention of making a career in the church and was rejected. His trade-family background was not acceptable. Thereafter his religious feelings were in turmoil; the church, Christianity itself, was like a magnet to him but he fought against believing any of it. He was once called "The village atheist".

The undoubted focus of the attraction was the uprising Cathedral, an easy journey from his home, which he first saw when he was twenty and which he described many times.

In their search for betterment the Hardy family and their aunt's family, the Sparks, tried by seeking professional advancement and by advantageous marriages. They were delighted when Thomas's sister Mary obtained a place at the Salisbury Teachers Training College in the Kings House, where royalty had stayed, set in a superior location on The Close bank of the river. Thomas himself took Mary there to begin her training. The fees were four pounds a term. Her first assessment described her as "backward" although she was so conscientious that she was soon given a scholarship and did not have to pay. But it was a poor place to learn anything. This was 1860 and teaching young women how to wash up dishes and keep the place spruce were considered just as important as instruction in art, needlework and literature. Several accounts were written by what you could only term "inmates" which set the establishment not that much higher than a home for difficult girls. One night Mary "escaped" and somehow got into the river. That sentence is almost the only firm reference to the happening and to the fact that after that night the Avon was out of bounds to students.

Hardy, who never forgot anything, and made use of such dramas although many years had gone by, has a sequence in 'Jude the Obscure' set in Salisbury, which is called Melchester, provoked by his sister's adventure.

Sue Bridehead, the main female character, likewise ends up in the river and, dragging herself out, staggers to the cottage door of Jude who, seeing her state, ushers her inside and helps her take off her wet clothes. Whether the soaked Mary ever had such succour is not known.

Jude is a dark character in a dark novel. Sue, his great love, is due to marry another man in Salisbury and, for the last time, the lovers meet. Jude is staying "in a little temperance hotel in a street leading from Salisbury Station." Hardy himself preferred The Red Lion.

On this last night they would be together, Jude the Obscure and Sue Bridehead get into St. Thomas's Church and there, at midnight and by candlelight, go through the pretence of a marriage service. When she leaves him she goes off to prepare for her real wedding.

It was in the same St. Thomas's Church on 9th July, 1974,

as part of the Salisbury Festival, a lady called Lois Deacon gave a lecture she called 'Thomas Hardy and the Salisbury See'. She had, with Terry Coleman, previously published a book called 'Providence and Mr. Hardy' which alleged that the novelist was, once more, and sensationally this time, borrowing from life for his fiction.

Even from his boyhood Hardy was frequently falling in love. He proposed to a Dorchester shop assistant but she turned him down and another of his impulsive love objects left the country. He had a clutch of comely cousins, the girls of his mother's sister Martha, and relationships in those days before widespread travel were sometimes kept barely legal within the family. Hardy fell in love with each of his cousins in turn and even, apparently, with his Aunt Martha. He was a born romantic.

His affair, if there was such a thing, with his pretty cousin Tryphena, his childhood playmate and the youngest of the girls, is a matter of conjecture. They were even said to have had a child. But Tryphena, like the others, made off. She married a man who ran a pub in Exeter, had four children and died before she was forty.

In their account Lois Deacon and Terry Coleman allege that Hardy and Tryphena were in a love relationship and that the night before Tryphena was to be married to another man, they went through a ghost marriage at midnight in St. Thomas's Church. Then, as the fictional Sue Bridehead did much later, she went off to don her wedding gown. Predictably this story set off a furore at the time and today it appears to be as near to fiction as anything Thomas Hardy ever wrote. When Tryphena died Hardy composed a touching poem about her. He called it: 'Thoughts of Phena' and he referred to her as his "lost prize"

"Not a line of her writing have I,
Not a thread of her hair."

But he did not go to her funeral.

⌐ↄ

Almost seventy years after Thomas Hardy's death in 1928 the BBC filmed a television version of one of his West Country stories – at The Walton Canonry, only yards from where his sister Mary had her drama in the Avon, whatever that drama was.

The story is called 'The Day after The Fair' and concerns a servant girl who meets a young upper-crust London man at a Wessex Fair. After a happy day together they end up in the hay. He has to return to London and they promise to exchange letters. The problem is – she cannot write. He is unaware of her background (they had little time for personal histories that carefree day) and is delighted when he receives a poetic love letter from her. But the letter is, in fact, written for the servant by the lady of the house, played in the television version by Hannah Gordon. The young man from London falls in love by post, but with the wrong woman.

The BBC decided that the perfect background for this typically Hardy bitter-sweet story was The Walton Canonry which was then the home of the enthusiastically unconforming Titled Family from whom we eventually bought it. They were provided with a temporary rented house and His Lordship and Her Ladyship and their ten lively children trooped off to live there while Thomas Hardy's story was unfolded before the cameras.

Filming a single scene can take hours or even days and it was sometimes late afternoon before the director and actors were getting to grips with the precise task. But at four o'clock on the first day two small children appeared, like a scene from their own melodrama, at the front gate and came shyly into the front garden.

"We're lost," complained one in a small but highly cultured voice. "We don't know where we live," said the second. Filming had to stop. The director groaned and the actors sat down. An escort was provided and the children were taken to their temporary home. They came back, sometimes three of them, on later afternoons.

We made our own film at The Walton Canonry. It was about ten years after the BBC had produced 'The Day after The Fair' and was a Christmas story – 'Present Spirits'. Matthew, our son, who had just left film school produced and directed it, Diana was co-producer and arranged accommodation for the cast – which included the leading actresses, Paula Wilcox and Sandra Dickinson. She also borrowed costumes from the Hampshire Museum and organised staff from a Salisbury hairdresser's to give up their Sunday to do the make up for the cast of forty for the final scene – a whole congregation of happy ghosts around a family sitting down to Christmas Dinner.

I wrote the script (and provided the finance) and dressed as a wordless red-coated ghost soldier as required. Everyone helped; a local choir sang carols and The Close Constable somehow shepherded an enormous 'cherry picker' crane under the arch of the main gate with an inch to spare.

It was the tale of a family who inherit an old house and decide to spend Christmas there – not knowing they will have the company of a collection of friendly ghosts – people who have lived in the house in the past. We had some professional child actors and my twin grandchildren Charlie and Joe played the sons of the family.

We filmed in February – aiming for someone (anyone!) to show the half-hour story the following Christmas. All we needed was snow – then it snowed! It snowed and snowed. Nobody could order a setting like that. Not in Salisbury anyway! It was a miracle.

'Present Spirits' was screened the following Christmas on Channel Four Television. We were very proud of it. It was a lovely film.

I was reminded of Hardy's ingenious story when we first moved into the Canonry. One week-end I found myself, rather unwillingly, in Stoke-on-Trent where I was to speak at a booksellers' lunch.

Families had special rates on Saturdays and Sundays at the hotel where I stayed. I recall going to the bar on the first evening and seeing three tiny infants sitting in a line on a large sofa, staring over the tops of dummies and each dressed in their 'jarmies'.

At the bar was a man who recognised me and made me an

offer – he would buy me a double scotch if I would write a love letter for him. I agreed. It was a letter of abject apology for some infidelity that Sharon had unearthed. Leaning on the bar I wrote the letter. I have to say, considering I had never met Sharon and had only just met Mike, it was not bad. It pleased Mike mightily. So much so that, having read it twice, he said: "Would you write one like that, this time for Angie . . . ? And then there's Kath . . ."

CHAPTER 20

The Masked Woman

Another of Salisbury Close's enduring mysteries is why one of the its most beautiful residents had to wear a mask. Her name was Charlotte Cradock and she lived with her mother and two equally comely sisters at Number 14, The Close. This was the early 18th Century and Salisbury had become a place known for its "quality" families and elegant entertainments. The Cradocks' pretty daughters lived in a world of genteel invitations, nights of theatre and music and gay dancing at The Assembly Rooms.

Along came Henry Fielding, who was to become one of the most feted authors of the time. He, like so many others, had a patron, James Harris, who lived at Malmesbury House, today still sitting exquisitely in its courtyard garden by the St. Ann's Gate, the man who had entertained Handel and heard him play the harpsichord. The house has a large sundial dating from those times and inscribed with Shakespeare's words from 'Hamlet' – "Life is but a walking shadow". Fielding had a reputation of being a somewhat dissolute man, his fine and fashionable clothes said to spend much of their time in the pawnshop. Neighbours in The Close recoiled from his London airs and graces, although it was not unknown for these to be followed by a visit from the bailiffs. Nor was he liked for his habit of inserting local people in his novels. The poisonous Dr Thwackum in 'Tom Jones' was said to be an outrageously unjust portrait of the devout Richard Hele, headmaster of the Cathedral School. But Fielding was an impressive presence, over six feet tall in an age of small men, he had a big face and what oddly seems to be a bigger nose. This is how he appears in one representation of him by Hogarth. Perhaps it was a fashion for artists to accentuate noses; John Constable and his friend Archdeacon John Fisher of Leadenhall are drawn with powerful noses; they could easily have been brothers.

Women and wine were Henry Fielding's interests; and in-fighting with his contemporary writers, Tobias Smollet and Samuel Richardson in particular. It did not take him long to fall in love with the delectable Charlotte Cradock, although he flirted around her sisters as well. If he had little money his reputation as a novelist and dramatist was growing. He made Charlotte the heroine, Sophia, of his most famous work 'Tom Jones', said to be the funniest novel in the English language. He courted her and married her in the autumn of 1734. Her mother was a widow and there was only a modest dowry of £1,500, so he must have been sincere.

They were said to have a "passionate marriage" but Fielding returned to rumbustious London at intervals, leaving Charlotte in Salisbury and there are sneaky accounts of his wild nights out. There was also a suspicion, borne out by later events, that he might have been seeking, and receiving, extra comforts nearer home.

Today there is scarcely a shred left of Charlotte's story – how she was thrown from an overturning carriage and how the wheel cruelly ran over her beautiful face. But, like Hardy in the next century, Henry Fielding was a writer who used everyday drama as his raw material, rarely wasting a scrap of real life. In his novel 'Amelia Booth', his heroine is unmistakably Charlotte as she was with certainty Sophia Weston in 'Tom Jones'. The fictional Amelia is also involved in a carriage accident which disfigures her. She has to wear a face mask for the rest of her life. So did Charlotte.

Although Salisbury people must have seen her in her disguise and known the cause, not a scrap of evidence apparently remains today. It could be one of those cases – like Hardy's embellished tales – where fiction has become enmeshed with clouded truth. On the other hand, the spiteful Samuel Richardson uttered a phrase about Fielding's wife's "noselessness" and Lady Louisa Stuart, a relative, writing years later, described "a frightful overturn which destroyed the gristle of her nose."

Dr. Edward Goldwyer lived next door to the Cradocks in The Close and this well-known surgeon is said to have operated on Charlotte's injuries. He also designed the mask that she wore for the rest of her short life. She died of consumption ten years after her marriage and Fielding was so distraught that he spent the entire night sobbing in the arms of his twenty-four year old housekeeper.

Two years later he married the housekeeper, Mary Daniel, who was then six months pregnant and was described loftily by Lady Stuart as with "few personal charms". The wedding was in one of the most insignificant London churches, St. Benet's in Thames Street, and was attended by a smattering of guests. Richardson had tart words to say and Smollet said Fielding had married "his own cook-wench".

Fielding, not to be outdone, declared "If you talk of virtue here's virtue! I married my whore yesterday." But Mary kept quiet and lived a long time, into the nineteenth century, long after Fielding or the others. She was a simple and kind woman and, in old age, she could be persuaded to tell stories of her marriage to a famous writer.

CHAPTER 21

Close Cures

SOME PEOPLE NEEDED TWO HANDS to lift the big brass knocker on the broad front door of our house. He was just on his second attempt when I untangled the many ancient chains inside and pulled it open. His eyes were bright behind his spectacles, he had neat grey hair, a good tweed suit with a club tie and brown boots. "Good morning," he said. "I would like to be your doctor." And so he was. Ignoring the possible breach of medical etiquette (soliciting custom is apparently not done), I agreed at once. He was like a Victorian doctor and he told engaging stories about The Close.

An elderly lady, a visitor staying with a friend in one of the big, old houses, came to his surgery one day suffering, he soon discovered, from shingles, an unpleasant and sometimes painful skin irritant. He prescribed the treatment and the following week saw the lady again at a sherry party being given by her hostess in The Close. The big room was crowded and the guests mostly elderly and deaf. Many were shouting. My doctor said to the lady of the house "How is your friend, Muriel, now?" "Muriel?" came the vague response. "She hasn't been very well. She has syphilis, you know." Seeing he looked so shocked she then bellowed over the hubbub of the room. "Muriel, where are you, dear?"

"Here," called Muriel from a noisy corner. "I'm here, Grace."

"You've got syphilis, haven't you?"

Muriel, deaf as the rest, shouted back: "Yes, dear. And it's a very bad dose this time!"

Medical men in Salisbury Close have frequently been notable, some notably eccentric. Bishop Seth Ward who restored the Palace and parts of the Cathedral and also built the College of Matrons, became weak of mind in his later years and, in Dora Robertson's words, became a goldmine to physicians and apothecaries. He was engrossed with alarming remedies for illnesses he never had and left behind details in a series of notebooks.

"Unguentum Podagricum (for the treatment of Gout) Take an old fat Cat and flea it, draw forth the Guts then with a rolling pin beat it wel, and putt it all together into the belly of a fat Gander with pepper, half a pound. Mustard and Parsley Seeds, six pennyweight of Bole Armoniac, a good quantity of Wormwood, Rue (and Garlic) Rost the Gander wel, saveing the greas, with it anoint the grieved part."

Gout might have been preferable.

Another recommended cure contained "handfuls of snails, worms," distilled in a gallon of Milk.

～✼～

A seventeenth century contemporary of Bishop Ward was a man who gained international fame for the treatment of eye-troubles. People sailed, with all that meant in those days, from far overseas for a consultation with Dr. D'Aubigny Turberville. There are tales of travellers arriving, not just at Southampton, the nearest port, but Tilbury and even Liverpool and asking hopefully: "How do I reach the eye doctor?"

Turberville was the first to use a magnet to extract a metal fragment from an eye. He used tobacco as a cure and tried untried operations for removing cataracts and even entire eyes. He ordained that his patients should wear a green silk dressing on their eyes. All manner of half and entirely blind people found their way to his house in The Close. One of his patients was Pepys, the diarist, who came from London with his bad sight, perhaps caused by writing late by candlelight. He called on Dr. Seth Ward as well and paid, while he was in Salisbury, a shepherd girl fourpence for leading his horse on the final stage of the journey to Stonehenge. His bill at The George Inn (despite silk sheets) did not please him, however: "Seven and six for bread and beer . . . I was mad."

Dr. Turberville's fame and success benefited not only the patients, and his bank account, but the hotel and lodging keepers of Salisbury. His biographer, Walter Pope, recorded "one could scarce peep out of doors, but he had a prospect of some led by Boys or Women, others with Bandages over one, or both Eyes and yet a greater number wearing green Silk upon their Faces . . . The Rendezvous of these Hoodwinked people was at the Doctor's House . . ."

Turverville's reputation never diminished. He even found a man who could only see in the dark and another whose sight was restored if the bridge of his nose was pinched.

On his memorial in the Cathedral is written:

> *"Beneath this stone, extinct he lies*
> *The only doctor for the eyes."*

⁓

Early doctors crossed many boundaries. Simon Foreman, in the sixteenth century, was known as a philosopher and astrologer but who filled in with bouts of carpentry and cutting overgrown hedges. He was also known as a prophet and progressed from this to what he called "nigromancy and the gift of calling on aungells". These angels apparently encouraged him to write a book of magick – he had already served a prison term for dabbling in it – and he was engrossed with the philosopher's stone. He became an usher at the school in Devizes but he continued to give strange advice to the citizens of The Close on their illnesses. He was not alone. Although not a doctor, Canon Leonard Bilson admitted defaming the Cathedral by carrying out "curious and forbidden acts" and performing "sorcery and magick". He twice ended up in the pillory, mocked and bombarded by a large crowd on Christmas Eve, 1560, no way for a man to start the festivities, and also served time in prison.

After a succession of odd, early doctors and their notions of medicine it was perhaps natural that when, much later, efforts to cure both smallpox and cholera, which visited the city regularly and left their deadly mark, were treated with suspicion.

William Goldwyre, father of the surgeon Edward who had operated on Charlotte Fielding after her carriage accident, was in the forefront of the movement to inoculate against smallpox. There was bitter opposition and the disease marched on. One outbreak in 1723 killed 165 citizens.

A relative of the Fielding family, Lady Mary Wortley Montagu had her own children inoculated with a controlled pox virus which she imported from Turkey. Then William Goldwyre carried out 44 inoculations at his house next to the Fieldings in The Close. Royalty became interested and George the First gave his leave for his grand-daughter to be inoculated – but not his grandsons who were too "valuable".

Suspicion and only partial success slowed the campaign until the end of the eighteenth century when cowpox vaccinations were introduced and the battle was won.

Dr. Andrew Middleton was probably Salisbury's greatest medical hero. Few people but he could, or would, understand that the city's mock title of "The English Venice" was killing its inhabitants; the open waterways and canals carried tons of disease every day. In 1832, March 21st was designated in the churches as 'A Day of Fasting and Humiliation on account of the spreading of the cholera'. Some people did not want to listen, despite the death count of 1849 – 192 in a few weeks. Naturally, those who listened least were those who were responsible financially for the upkeep of the waterways. They were going to have to pay for the system to be ended.

The surgeon, Middleton, never gave up. He tramped through dwellings knee high in sewage with dying children huddled in a filthy back room. It was he who told the story of the diggers who thought they had found a medicinal spring when what they had done was pierced a cess-pit.

Against continuing opposition from the tight-fisted and ignorant, Andrew Middleton never surrendered. Eventually the canals and odious waterways were drained and filled in. Fresh drinking water from the River Bourne was pumped into the city. The cholera retreated, the terrible death rate diminished. People began to realise the truth.

At the end of it Middleton wrote: "I shall always be happy to plead guilty to any charge of having caused the destruction of the English Venice since by that destruction New Salisbury has been created and very many hundreds of human beings saved from untimely death".

To be a doctor in The Close was usually a rewarding position. Its inhabitants were often rich, elderly and prone to complaints. One modern general practitioner showed me a rather sombre scrapbook he had been keeping. It contained the obituaries from 'The Times' of all his famous patients who had passed away over the years. Politicians, statesmen, and several well-known scoundrels, they were all there. When Edward Heath rather courageously, but not untypically, took himself off to Baghdad to ask Saddam Hussein for the release of a group of British hostages who had fallen into his hands, the one-time prime minister did not crowd the plane with advisers or negotiators. He took with him his local doctor from Salisbury, practically hi-jacking him from his surgery at short notice. At one moment the young man had been feeling pulses, the next he was feeling nervous. Heath wanted to make sure that when he came face to face with the Iraqi villain he was fit and well enough to sustain an argument. He and the doctor got the people out.

Dr. William Goldwyre, Henry Fielding's neighbour in The Close, was the only known holder of a key to the St. Ann's Gate. This was so he could be called quickly to his patients in the night. He was famous for "the good which he is known to do in the exercise of his calling, particularly in the Case of cutting for the Stone".

There was another doctor, Henry Hele who for years held his surgery within a two minute walk of where I am writing this, and whose family, particularly his brother Richard, were so highly held in the community that they were provided with a "whole seat" in the Cathedral provided none of the other distinguished worshippers were inconvenienced. He was also permitted "at his own expense, to put on a door and lock up the said Seat". He died in July 1756 and had requested that he be carried to his grave as early in the morning as convenient, his body to be borne by "six ancient poor men." He left his Hebrew Bible to the Cathedral School.

CHAPTER 22

Scruff Golding

To some of his fellow teachers and universally to his pupils he was known as Scruff. Big as a haystack and with less order; there was little way of distinguishing between his overgrown hair and his overgrown beard. He dressed in shabby clothes. Except on Wednesdays. Then he became a sailor. Trimmed and scrubbed, his officer's uniform sharp and his manner commanding, he prepared from early morning to take his crew out into the grey and mysterious sea – The local River Solent.

William Golding wrote his revolutionary novel 'Lord of The Flies' and won the Nobel Prize for Literature. It was an amazing thing because he had comparatively little written work behind him. He was inward and awkward, losing himself in the corridors of Bishop Wordsworth's School, in

The Salisbury Cathedral Close, and in life itself. His sternest critic – apart from himself – was his contemporary, Anthony Burgess, who wrote volumes and never won the Nobel Prize. When Golding died, an old man, Burgess put together one of the meanest obituaries I have ever read. It reeked of envy. In it he pointed out, not for the first time, that it would not be possible to start a fire with a lens from a pair of spectacles as happens in 'Lord of The Flies''. What a damning revelation! Not that Golding would have cared. He did not appear to care about much, although this might be another harsh judgement. He liked mumbling in Greek, playing chess and the oboe, and he loved the sea like a brother.

During the Second World War he had spent four years in the navy and he was reluctant to let the tides ebb. In a school photograph he sits like a uniformed captain among his crew. Eagerly he awaited Wednesday when he could be free from teaching the boys their native language and take them down to the military port of Marchwood, near Southampton. Smallish Army ships sail from Marchwood to some of the world's more remote harbours, islands and creeks where soldiers are camped. Lieutenant Golding never attempted that distance. His crew rowed out into the grey Solent with him in the stern, scanning the horizon. His navigation, however, seems to have been on a level with his imagination. Twice the whaler and its crew had to be rescued from mud-banks.

But he was a great, unusual, man. He almost stumbled about the school in a sagging sports jacket, sloppy grey flannels and unkempt shoes. He was not an outwardly happy person: you could not imagine him guffawing. But one of the most joyous pieces of television film I have ever seen is him galloping wildly towards the camera on a huge horse in a field. He seems as big and hairy as the horse.

He wrote almost in secret, in odd corners of the staff room, by hand, or by retreating to some niche to bang fiercely on a massive typewriter. Many of his pupils recall him appearing in class with an armful of manuscript and distributing it around the desks with instructions for his pupils to count the words. The power and success of his writing seemed to wash over him. He hated to see his books in the shops (the first and only author, I imagine, to have complained about that). He would buy one of his books and take it home and burn it. He once went into Beech's second hand bookshop just outside the North Gate of The Close and bought a paperback of some of his poetry so he could add it to his living room fire. At the same time he spotted a book by a fellow teacher in the One-Shilling rack and transferred it to the Sixpenny section.

Music was his second interest. He played the oboe (once under the baton of Sir Adrian Boult) and various other instruments and he had a good tenor voice. The oboe being the instrument used for a single note when an orchestra is tuning before playing, he privately enjoyed his brief moments of musical glory. At one rehearsal he had sounded the note and the conductor asked: "Mr. Golding, can you give us that 'A' again." The shaggy man lifted his instrument but – a stickler for the English language – first pointed out. "I cannot give you that one, but I'll give you one like it." He was not someone to court popularity.

He went to Bishop's Wordsworth's for a short time before the Second World War and his naval service. He returned with the peace, a large, untidy and incongruous figure in the staff room full of men in stiff demob suits and shiny shoes.

Determined not to leave his maritime life completely adrift he built a lifeboat in the garden of his house, then in London Road, Salisbury, but was unable to move it out. He had to hire a crane.

It was not untypical of William Golding, with his innate modesty and general carelessness, that he should not begin to write an autobiography until he was eighty-one in 1992, a few months before he died. He left behind a handful of pages, quite a lot of which, he readily confessed, were probably not true. The records of a life in which much had happened were scrappy and in the main unrevised. He said of himself that he was probably writing "a memory of a memory." Some of the stories said to be authentic cannot be so, since they occurred before his birth in 1911. As an infant he claims to have witnessed a First World War naval action in the Bristol Channel, as seen from his grandmother's house; three British warships sinking a German submarine with depth charges. According to naval records it did not happen.

There are shadowy descriptions of his parents' house at Marlborough which he "feared" and Sunday walks in Savernake Forest. But the scrappy story rarely gets beyond childhood. He was apparently very proud of a new pair of small shoes which provokes a revealing remark: "It sorts ill with my lifelong irritation with being smart or tidy or, if the truth be told, clean. I am only clean when it occurs to me that

I would be more comfortable if I had a bath or a wash . . ."
  So there.

⁓

It is the recollections of his pupils that paint a fuller and in the most part affectionate picture. His battered black car, streaked with white mud (he eventually lived at Broadchalke a few miles from Salisbury) coming through the gate in The Close Wall; the happy picture of him at the Market Fair, walking with his family, his great whiskery face further decorated with orange candyfloss; his perpetual pacing in class said to be his relic of his days at sea. He may well have been muttering in Greek while his pupils scanned his latest fictional manuscript for typing errors. Some boys used to bet on how far he paced during a lesson, meticulously counting each step.

There was a lot of natural speculation as to which of his pupils ended up as characters in 'Lord of The Flies'. Any fat lad was automatically saddled with being Piggy but there were few other claims. The truth was, Golding remembered very few of the boys he had taught. To him, he admitted, they were just a sea of faces.

People said he was more of an educator than a teacher but he was quite frank about it – it was a job he quit as soon as he realised he could make more money from writing. He made sincere friends, especially through music, including Iona Brown, a beautiful young woman, a singularly talented violinist and conductor, who often graced Sir Edward Heath's gatherings and who died too young. She called Golding her second father.

William Golding made comparatively little of his achievements. He went to lecture in America because the money was good.

There is a plaque and a William Golding award for Creative Writing instigated at Bishop Wordsworth's, but the man who won the Nobel Prize for Literature is remembered mainly by such as the pupil who came to see him in the staff room for an oboe lesson. Golding was engrossed in a game of chess. Vaguely he looked at the arriving boy and the instrument and then down at his chess pieces. "Go to the music room," he said to the lad. "Put it together and blow. I'll be along soon."

CHAPTER 23

Ted

EDWARD HEATH WAS NOT TO everyone's taste. Like him or loathe him, in a place like Salisbury Cathedral Close, which for centuries has accommodated many famous, and sometimes thoroughly odd, characters he was completely at home, one of the notable residents of the twentieth century. Even today, five years after his death, if you mention to anyone that you have lived in The Close the next enquiry frequently goes: "Did you know Ted Heath?" Sometimes even "*Do* you know Ted Heath?"

As far as Sir Edward loved anything he loved his ancient and daintily trim house, Arundells, with its clipped lawns and precise flower beds sloping to the Avon at the rear, its unique view of the Cathedral and his own security guards clustered at the front. It was the first time, he recalls with brisk brevity in his autobiography, 'The Course of My Life', that he had known a home of his own. The Salisbury Member of Parliament, Robert Key, told him about Arundells and "it was love at first sight". It was one of the original canon's houses of The Close, (afterwards the residence of a cleric deprived of it for practising witchcraft in the sixteenth century) but with many alterations, one of which was the removal of a Victorian ballroom. "I was pleased about that," Sir Edward once confided in me. "It's a difficult thing, dancing by yourself."

He would have needed to do so for he was a lonely man. Away from London he would take walks, accompanied by a minder, armed and unspeaking, and was often to be found in inns and pubs around Salisbury, sitting silently in a corner. He had adopted a sort of round-the-city timetable, visiting pubs clockwise, over a period. Sometimes he would turn up to sign copies of 'The Course of My Life' stacked on the bar. On the evening of the day his knighthood was announced we met him sitting wordlessly with his security man in a pub at Wilton. Every year he would invite all the pub landladies to lunch at Arundells. His customary solitariness naturally provoked rumour about his private life. When he was eighty the BBC sent a television team down to interview his neighbours. The first question the producer asked me was: "Is Ted Heath gay?"

"No," I said. "He's bloody miserable."

He was not someone you could ask questions of, although I did ask him once what he thought of a notorious Tory MP. He did not hesitate: "Crook, crook, crook," he snorted. "Three times a crook."

But once I went to the local radio studio in Salisbury and found the rotund and famous man padding about in his stockinged feet. I think it was because it was a small studio and he had been told to 'Keep Quiet'.

By all accounts, including those of the crews from Poole Harbour who sailed with him on his yacht 'Morning Cloud' he was a fearless and skilful man in the most stormy sea. The only time I saw him register sorrow was when he was talking about that night when the vessel came to grief in a Channel gale. He was not aboard but his godson was one of the two men lost. As he told the tale he began to cry. He gave up sailing because, as he said, he could not afford it "under this government" which was Tory. But he loved going about The Close in a huge sailing shirt of blue and white horizontal stripes, like a full-blown spinnaker. If he was invited to some social event in the neighbourhood he would frequently reply that he would not be able to accept, and then perversely turn up in his spinnaker shirt among the nicely dressed guests.

You could see what he was like at school at Broadstairs in Kent. Clever and sarcastic and no stranger to the tuck-shop. He liked my wife Diana especially because, at parties, she made sure his plate and his glass did not stay unoccupied for long. We first met him at a dinner in someone's house. He came in unapologetically late (as he frequently did) but properly turned out, and sat next to my wife. She is an interesting person but she scarcely had time to speak to him because he promptly dozed off. He was even snoring. He awoke after a few minutes and became affable. We ended the evening singing Christmas carols in front of the fire. These naps were a curious (and I think deliberate) habit of Ted's. He would pose happily for a photograph with visitors in his house but fall fast asleep in the midst of them before the picture could be taken. Often I wondered why the photographer did not press the button anyway. It would have made a good picture. But he never did.

One evening we were at a musical evening in the Medieval Hall and Ted was sitting next to Diana in the front row. He held a glass of malt whisky but even this did not prevent him dropping off to sleep. He slowly lurched forward and my wife caught the tumbler (the glass, not Sir Edward) before it hit the ground.

He was caustic about the mulled wine often served in some clergy homes at Winter gatherings. Was it supposed to be more religiously acceptable than un-mulled wine? Or Scotch?

We once had a cricket match where Ted, a famously enthusiastic musical conductor, relieved the bandmaster of a local silver band of his baton and in our garden conducted the musicians in The Helston Floral Dance. The band still talk about it. On that occasion we had a bottle of scotch concealed in the greenhouse with instructions to the gardener to keep the ex-prime minister replenished.

Musical people have told me that, for all his eagerness, Ted was not very adept as a conductor. Once at the Edinburgh Festival he was allowed to conduct a famous orchestra, which pleased him immensely. It was only for an overture – something which apparently the players knew so well they could perform it with their eyes closed.

Robert Key, the Salisbury Member of Parliament for twenty-five years and who told Ted about Arundells, is an expansive man in every sense of the word. He was the rotund Heath's Private Parliamentary Secretary once and the pair of them in close conference would have been enough to block the light. Mr. Key, the most amiable of people and highly popular in the constituency where he was born (in the Walton Canonry) is also vocally musical. Each time he was returned to Westminster at an election he stood on the balcony of the old White Hart Hotel and sang a fine, loud song called 'The Fly Be On The Turnip'. He abandoned his deep Houses of Parliament accent and took on the Dorset voice of Bill Scroggins, whose life, according to the song, was devoted to hoeing turnips. 'The Fly Be On The Turnip' would be appreciated by Thomas Hardy or William Barnes, the vernacular poet. It is also the marching song of the one-time Dorset Regiment.

> "*The vly, the vly, the vly be on the turmut,*
> *An' 'tis all me eye vur I to try*
> *To keep vlies off the turmuts.*"

A large figure, Robert was appointed Minister of Highways in the Conservative Government. He was nicknamed "The Colossus of Roads".

It was a strange thing that in a serene and set place like The Close, Sir Edward Heath's security guards, uniformed and sub-machine-gun-armed, seemed, after a while, to fit almost unnoticed into the staid landscape. There was a group of more than half a dozen and some residents wondered how necessary they were but Ted himself was aware of the risks to even a former prime minister. He told me that there had been two attempts on his life.

The men worked in shifts from their strongpoint, a block-house built inside the curly iron gates of his house. These days it is used as a reception area for visitors to the house and there were seven thousand of them in the first few months of it opening as a museum. In the former days at least one man used to sit in front of a bank of television screens, pinpointing different aspects of the house and its approaches. There was also usually one screen showing Coronation Street or the Test Match. We got to know these guardians. One would knock on our door and ask me to give a signed book for a charity auction. He would have a cup of coffee in the kitchen with his sub-machine gun draped across the table. After a while you hardly noticed it but I sometimes used to think what a strange world it was.

Everyone took Ted's health seriously. There were the normal Close Constables on the gate (after Ted died one of his security team joined them) and Arundells was like a redoubt. The first week we lived in The Close I went to the newsagents in the town to order some deliveries. I was wearing my old "gardening" clothes, although I rarely did any, and the newsagent looked me up and down. "We have to be careful about deliveries in The Close," he said. "It's all the VIPs who live there. Are you working at The Walton Canonry?" I told him, truthfully, that I was starting the next day.

But there were times when I thought the security was a trifle casual. One Sunday I was about to pass Arundells when I saw Tom King, then Minister for Northern Ireland (and this was at the height of The Troubles), peering under the bonnet of his Mercedes parked outside Edward Heath's gate. He had obviously been staying the night at Arundells and could not start his car. I've had quite elderly Mercedes for years and I've never known one to fail to start first time. Mr. King was engaged in some badinage with the guard at the gate, something on the lines of: "You should get a British car, sir." But it seemed to me a dangerous situation, a cabinet minister looking below the hood because a prime car does not start outside a former premier's gate. I took a detour fairly quickly, I have to say, half expecting to hear a loud bang at any moment. It did not happen. They must have known what they were about.

If the many melancholies of older life visited Sir Edward Heath, and I am sure they did, he compensated for them with moments of optimism and humour left over from his schooldays. These private and often puzzling jokes would be accompanied by a huge but mainly silent guffaw, the pink face would become pinker, his eyes would water and he would emit a wheezing sound, both shoulders going up and down like a pump.

"I am told I have the cholesterol of a forty-year-old." He once exclaimed to me almost joyfully. On another occasion, after I had written an article for the 'Daily Mail', I was walking my dog and his car slowly drove by. He wound down the back window and bellowed: "I see you are in the Public Prints again!"

Among his few friends were, curiously, Harold and Mary Wilson. One sleety winter's morning I saw Ted, enveloped in a mountainous overcoat, leaving home on his way to his old political rival's funeral in the Isles of Scilly. Not long afterwards Lady Wilson visited him at Arundells.

I asked him if he would be chairman at a Foyles Literary Luncheon in London where I was to be guest of honour, and although he had a loaded diary he wiped it clean and came. Christina Foyle said that it was the best lunch she had organised since beginning in 1930, six months before I was born. The list of speakers since then reads like a Who's Who of the World. Previously I had been a guest at these regular occasions (it was a popular event and excellent value for money. On another strange occasion I replaced Kingsley Amis as guest of honour. As I entered the hotel in Park Lane Christina Foyle, then in her late eighties, approached and said in her high-class voice: "Leslie, will you please replace Kingsley Amis today. He is not well." I agreed to do so. "Is he very ill?" I asked. "Very." She looked at me directly. "In fact, he's dead."

Guiltily occupying Kingsley's seat I told a few stories about the famous novelist. After the lunch, going out into the street, I saw his death announced on the front of 'The Evening Standard'. So, of course, did everyone else.

Ted Heath was a good speaker – not so much for what he said as for what he did not say. His pauses were as long and loaded as anything Harold Pinter ever wrote. I was once at an expansive dinner in London when he was holding forth. I was sitting at a table with Denis Thatcher, another exceptionally individual man. Sir Edward was no admirer of Margaret Thatcher, of course, and she was then Prime Minister. As part of his speech, Ted was mentioning various notable guests: "And, of course, Mr Denis Thatche" he said. There came a pause, stretched to the limit. Then " . . . that brave man."

I swear he had never read a word of my novel which we were celebrating at the Foyles Lunch (I forget which one it was) but he held forth, making everyone laugh, for twenty minutes. "The Thomases throw the best parties in Salisbury Cathedral Close," he said. "They always serve champagne."

It had been a jolly occasion. As Ted left talking to the former Labour minister, Roy Hattersley, I heard him say: "Let's go to The House and have another laugh down there."

When we had left The Walton Canonry for a house overlooking the harbour at Lymington, we returned for some event at Salisbury Cathedral and seeing Sir Edward Heath there invited him to Sunday Lunch at our new home. We were thinking a few weeks, even a month or two ahead, but the following morning the telephone rang. It was Ted: "Will this Sunday be all right?"

He came with two security men who locked the car out of sight and then disappeared. At the table he began, unasked, to tell the story of how he had brought Chi-Chi, the Giant Panda, from China to the London Zoo – an enchanting tale.

Diana had gone to the harbour and bought half a dozen fresh lobsters. But the fisherman who had just caught them was no admirer of the ex-Prime Minister. "Ted Heath!" he snorted. "Him! Ruined the British fishing industry . . ." He still sold us the lobster. When our guests were tucking into them I said to Ted: "The fisherman who caught these is no great fan of yours . . ." Ted, who was an avid eater, dug deeper into the shell. "Jolly fine lobster, though," he said.

Every year the Residents of The Close have a Christmas party to which you bring your own food. It is never less than a lively affair and six months after returning and buying De Vaux House we were glad to re-new our acquaintance with many of the people we had known there. There was a conjuror and a lively irreverent, Gentleman Chorister who sang versions of Christmas carols

> *"It came upon the midnight clear*
> *That well-known yell of old*
> *'I'm stuck outside without my key*
> *I'm drunk and tired and cold . . .'"*

After leading the chorus the reverend had to dash across The Close for the rehearsal of the genuine Cathedral Carol Service due the following night. In an hour he was back and singing with us:

> *"I saw three cars come speeding in*
> *On Christmas Day, on Christmas Day*
> *They crashed into my wheelie bin*
> *On Christmas Day in the morning."*

It was at this cheery gathering that I met a lady called Pamella who had been Sir Edward's housekeeper at Arundells. She was a surprising person, a Caribbean Londoner who told me she had held the former Prime Minister's hand when he was dying.

After he had died the house became a museum and Pamella and Stuart, the gardener, show around hundreds of visitors, still curious about Ted Heath, the different man.

The house still stands with odd daintiness behind its big gates. There are many visitors. But Ted is not at home.

As well as being a famous place of worship, a soaring beauty spot and loaded with history, Salisbury Cathedral is known to the police as an occasional and (needless to say) unusual crime scene. Most, but not all, of the incidents are minor and a number are curious. One of the helpers, working at the desk where visitors pay their voluntary subscriptions before entering the sacred building, found that her handbag had been stolen. The area is covered by CCTV cameras and a search of the film revealed the petty crime being committed.

Sadly only a stringy hand was portrayed. The rest of the malefactor was never exposed.

There was also the case of the verger's verge. The verge is a wooden baton which, from ancient times, has given a Cathedral verger his authority. This one was stolen during a service only to re-appear two years later in the same place, perhaps a case of difficulty in disposing of it or a jolt of conscience.

The Cathedral shop, adjoining the Refectory has, perhaps surprisingly, its own share of shoplifters. The favourite objects for theft are *rosary beads*. So many have been stolen that they are now displayed right next to the till where the staff can keep a close eye on them.

But one crime was as huge and heartless as it was audacious. In the year after the terrifying Tsunami had drowned huge areas of Asia and many people, a service of commemoration was held in Salisbury Cathedral. There was a large congregation – and a large collection was taken. The money bags were gathered and blessed, whereupon two men appeared calmly wheeling an invalid chair which seemed to add to their authenticity. The bags were placed in boxes which were loaded on the chair which was then blessed again and wheeled away with ceremony through the hundreds of onlookers, and out of the Cathedral – never to be seen again.

By the time anyone thought to ask: "Where has the collection gone?" it had vanished. The invalid chair was later found abandoned nearby. Today you can see it parked in its accustomed place just inside the door from the Cloisters. Nothing else has ever been recovered.

~

The Cathedral has suffered other losses, more through care-lessness than crime. One morning in the 1990s 'The Times' contained a lengthy news story, accompanied by a photograph of the spire and a somewhat bashful member of the Deanery staff. It related that the Cathedral had found itself in possession of £800,000 from leases, rents, school fees, and other sources, a nice sum in the bank. It was decided that having this huge sum hanging around even for a short time was not good economics. So it was invested – unfortu-nately in a company called BCCI which, the following day slid spectacularly into a very large, black, bottomless hole.

There were timid old ladies living in The Close who had heard the crash was coming and deftly withdrew their investments.

~

The American woman tourist took in the wide and lofty Nave, peered beyond the Choir to the High Altar with its distant glimmering window and said: "This must surely take some Spring Cleaning." She was right. In times past keeping the huge place clean and polished was the task of a group known, rather ungallantly, by the rest of the Cathedral hierarchy as The Closet Women. Today the tasks are tackled by a more genteel set of volunteer ladies who call themselves The Holy Dusters.

Another busy lady around the Cathedral is the widow of one of the greatest men I have ever known – Jim Laker who once won a cricket Test Match against Australia more or less on his own. He took nineteen of the twenty wickets needed to win the game for England, a feat that had never before been accomplished and unlikely to be again.

After his triumph in the north, he modestly got into his car and drove home, stopping for a pint and a sandwich in a pub. The highlights of the astonishing day's play in the Test Match were being shown on television and he sat with the barman watching and talking. The barman never realised who he was.

Although he played cricket for Surrey and, at the end of his career, for Essex, Jim was a gently spoken Yorkshireman, a rarity in itself. Stories are one of cricket's great attractions and he told a good story. "Playing in India once," he ruminated. "I was just running into bowl, just about to let go of the ball, when I saw a great rat on the pitch. It was sitting there between me and the batsman. Huge. At that moment a big shadow fell. The cricketers looked up. It was one of the great, ghostly kites, the scavenger hawks that circle slowly above Indian towns. It more or less fell on the rat and swooped away with it in its claws. After a bit, we went on playing" said Jim.

Lily is Austrian (and a Scrabble Champion in English) and when she met Jim just after the war she was working for the Bishop of London. "I asked her where she worked" recalled Jim. "And she told me it was Fulham Palace." He grinned. "I thought it was a dance hall."

Lily Laker has just turned ninety. She swims three times a week and walks almost everywhere. She also does a passable imitation of Jim's bowling action. One of the few difficulties she had as the wife of a famous England bowler was the wintertime dinners. "There were many and I cannot stand to eat chicken – or any bird for that matter. And it was always chicken. I used to wait until no one was looking and wrap up my chicken and pass it to Jim under the table." She moved into a courtyard apartment just outside the Cathedral Close one year after her husband's death 23 years ago. "I knew it was right for me," she said. "I said I would take it right away. It was Jim's birthday.

One of The Holy Dusters was a forthright – and to me at first, rather frightening lady – called Helen Foley. She firmly believed that The Close should be the preserve of the residents ("Our garden." She would claim) and festivals, concerts and, particularly, firework displays were to be abhorred. Even some incomers . . .

"A pornographer has come among us!" She exclaimed Biblically as soon as I arrived. But we became friends and I found she had a story to tell. In the nineteen thirties she was the young wife of a District Officer in the Anglo-Egyptian Sudan. Her husband's area of responsibility was huge – about the size of Wales – and he used to go off on his tours of inspection on a camel. "He would sit facing backwards" she recalled. "Leaning against the hump – so he could read a book as he travelled."

She composed her own book called 'Letters to My Mother' – written while she was working with the wartime Red Cross in the Sudan. 'An aeroplane coming from the West force landed somewhere out in nowhere . . . An old man tending his goats came by and was very curious. 'Good God,' he said. 'I've seen these things flying over but I thought they were this size.' He crossed his fingers to look like an aeroplane. Then he said. 'Is it male or female?'

I tried to interest a publisher in the collection but they did not think there was any profit in it. More's the pity. She had it published privately in the end.

When she was on one of her long visits to Salisbury Close from Washington D.C. Priscilla Tapley picked up her household cleaning materials and joined The Holy Dusters. While he was able, her husband, James Leroy Tapley, used to make the journey also. He was a movie-like Southern gentleman born in Shaw, in a corner of Bolivar County in the Mississippi Delta. It was "a relative backwater, in a society that was parochial, stratified, old fashioned, stable and determined to stay that way," as he put it in his autobiography published shortly before he died. It is Jim Tapley's voice I still remember, that accent, drawling but loud, full of enthusiasm and fun. He was a railroad lawyer in the South and he had endless stories from the Delta, "flat as the eye can see . . . A place where the Mississippi frequently flooded over the levels built to contain it, a land of bear, snake and panther, Choctaw and Chickasaw Indians." But somehow like his wife, at one time a librarian, he fitted into the Englishness of The Close.

Priscilla knew almost every one of the inhabitants and was full of the history. She has a good eye for the local oddities. "I walked into the Nave one morning and saw a camel walking through it, heading for the Font which it drank dry in almost one swallow." The camel is half a world from that mentioned by Helen Foley. It belongs to the Countess of Chichester and is used to appearing in Christmas Pageants where it lends a touch of Eastern authenticity. On other days it can be seen carrying children around the village where Lady Chichester lives.

I had never seen a font like they had in the Cathedral. You could hear it. It murmured and gurgled and the water sometimes made a sort of music. It must have been fun to be christened in it. But it was only one of a series of fonts stretching back two centuries. It was followed by an even more revolutionary design by William Pye who is known appropriately as a water sculptor.

This was brought in on a truck and edged down the length of the Cathedral, watched by the Dean June Osborne, who has been among those nursing the project for years. It is different, there is no doubt about that. Some people think it is too different. But it seems to me that for all its Star Trek look it fits among its ancient surroundings. It is comfortable and it seems to know it. It is the first permanent font in more than a century of baptisms. Not since 1890 has there been a place of baptism with security of tenure. In that year the original font, sitting usefully in its appointed place was uprooted and retired – to Australia.

If you happen to be in Yankalilla, fifty miles north of Adelaide, and are aware of it, the original Salisbury font is in the church there. Christchurch holds a hundred people and the font is its prize possession. People bring photographs of the alabaster traveller to England and bring them to Salisbury.

⁓

Diana Reader Harris was one of the most beautiful women you could ever see. She was beyond eighty, tall, slenderly elegant and totally blind. She lived in an old house next to Choristers Green across the road from Ted Heath, with a companion, her widowed sister-in-law I believe, called Henrietta, but known simply as 'H'. Unfortunately 'H' had a speech impediment and she was unable to pronounce the single letter of her nickname. Diana was once the renowned headmistress of Sherborne Girls' School in Dorset. Although she could not see, she had the gift of knowing certain people by their presence. "Is that you, Leslie?" she used to ask in a crowded room and knowing it was. And I did not even have to speak.

"Come and sit by me." She would say. "Tell me what you've been doing."

She told me that on some evenings, before she went to bed, she would get 'H' to read a chapter from one of my books. I always hoped, and imagined, she meant a travel book or one of the other non-fiction works and not some steamy excerpt from one of my novels. I did not dare ask her and all she would say was: "They do make us laugh."

⁓

The two hundred and fifty or so residents of The Close have their own vicar. When we lived there it was Canon Phillip Roberts, an Australian who had soldiered in New Guinea during the war, and was good at stories. "When I was at a parish in London," he said. "I got to know John Betjeman. He was terrified of dying and when he was going in that direction I went to visit him. He was in bed and I asked him if he would like to receive Communion. "What, here?" he asked.

"Here," I said. "You can receive the Sacrament anywhere." He agreed and I found an ironing board and set it up at his bedside. Using that as an altar table I gave him the bread and the wine. It was odd but it seemed to give him some comfort."

Quite a lot of the earlier residents of The Close – who in those days were referred to as The Quality – vied with each other, as motorists do today, with the smartness of their carriages. People would wait at the gates to see the conveyances enter or exit, to take note of the number and the fineness of the horses, and the grooms' apparel.

Few of the clergy had such aspirations, or money. There was a Canon Bouverie who arrived to live in The Close with all his household goods piled on an ox-wagon.

Eccentricity was almost expected of the choral vicars and the other denizens of the cathedral. Once established they could choose and adopt a style of life impossible for a parish. Although there were services several times a day, there were times when it was difficult to find someone to officiate at them. Even then the service was often held in a mumble and some of the canons sang hideously out of tune. The choir learned to sing doggedly over them. Archdeacon Honey would arrive at evensong with a picnic basket and insert himself in a curtained snug where, during the sermon, he worked his way through a pile of sandwiches produced from a newspaper wrapping, or sometimes a slice of pie, and a half bottle of port.

Most stayed as long as they could, their oddities tolerated, even expected, until they drifted muttering into old age. Dean Hamilton stayed for thirty years in his post and eventually had to be transported to services in a bath chair. He would wrap curtains around him to ward off draughts and was a virtually invisible figure to the congregation, only identified by his thin and ghostily wailing voice. A sub-dean, known to the choirboys as Snipey was stone deaf and carried a huge silver ear trumpet which he often dropped during the quietest prayers. Another vicar always removed his false teeth and placed them on top of his stall where they grinned at the worshippers in the front pews.

Apart from these diversions, the heating of the Cathedral was limited to three huge braziers all in the choir area. The rest of the Cathedral was starkly cold. People brought horse blankets with them. The braziers were large and fierce often spewing flames and ash and smoke, causing coughs and streaming eyes.

These were Dora Robertson's observations on the Cathedral as it was in the late nineteenth century. She also notes succinctly that of £900 in the bank account of the choristers £500 had been mysteriously invested in consoles. The choristers continued to be poorly treated. They were supposed to be educated as well as being able to sing, but often their Tutors appeared unaware of this or simply ignored the requirement. Sometimes the boys would go for days or weeks without any instruction, being left to their own devices in the classroom, having fights and keeping pets. One class kept a jackdaw captive in a stove meant to heat their classroom but which was never used, even on the most bitter winter's day. Often the boys were grossly ill-treated. One master used his cane violently at any excuse while his daughter shouted: "Flog 'em pa!" Their tutor scarcely got from his bed where he was nursing a foot throbbing with gout.

There were small compensations; the tradition of spur-money continued well into the nineteenth century. One choirboy was cheeky enough to challenge the Duke of Wellington, England's most famous man, when he clanked into the Cathedral in his spurs. At least he had left his horse outside the door which was not always the case. The Duke, after the first surprise, agreed good-humouredly to pay a fee (more than the sixpence demanded) and ordered his entourage to pay up likewise. It was a profitable day for the boys.

Extraordinarily a holiday was given regularly so the choir could visit Salisbury Races and each boy was given a shilling out of church funds to finance his betting.

The treatment meted out in the choir-school was probably no worse and no better than in a good many Victorian schools. Tom Brown's experiences were widespread. But the choristers had the added misery of being roused roughly at unearthly hours to sing at services which few others attended. They would troop back to a meagre breakfast eaten at the same table as a master filling himself up with bacon, kidneys and eggs, and totally oblivious of their twitching noses. Main meals for the boys were rough, often offal which lurking dogs below the table rejected with a sniff.

Some of the punishments within the school, committed by boys on other boys were worse than any official sanctions. A dropped catch or a moment of careless fielding on the cricket pitch could result in retribution on the end of a cricket stump. Wet and knotted towels were used as lashes to beat shivering naked newcomers in an initiation ritual.

There is today to be seen in the Cathedral a stone worn with an oval depression made, it is said, by the heads of choirboys banged on it as a greeting to the school. They still do it, but in a token ceremonial. The newly arrived girl choristers are patted on their heads with a Bible.

John Harding, a nine-year old from Mere, a village not distant from Salisbury, became a choirboy in the early nineteenth century (taking the place of a lad who had been stabbed during a fight). Normally a prospective singer would have had to wait until there was a natural vacancy (an older chorister's voice had broken) but Harding was ushered in hurriedly and stayed, in one connection or another, for more than sixty years. He left a record of his time at the Cathedral, good and bad, but he not only survived he relived it with some pleasure.

The happier times of the early twentieth century were broken by first one war and then another. The Cathedral still held its processions and sang its anthems. Today a service at Christmas or on Easter Day still sees every seat (there are no longer pews in the nave) taken. And there are still quirky moments occurring at the most solemn times. Some of the

Holy Duster ladies recall hearing a small, sing-song voice coming from one of the enclosed, private chapels. They crept in and saw a young boy standing before the altar, blowing out the devotional candles and tunefully chanting: "Happy birthday to you . . . Happy birthday to you . . .

Characters are still to be seen and talked about. Sarah Stancliffe, the energetic wife of the Bishop, often does her rounds by bike. One day she approached me at speed as I was walking, and with her legs thrust out horizontally each side. "Wheeee!" she cried exultantly. "Wheeeee!"

She said: "I do that to amuse my grand-children."

Then, one evening, Princess Margaret appeared as guest of honour at a party in one of the Close houses. A jolly time was had by all, especially the princess and by the exuberant Mrs. Olga Corey. When the small and rounded Mrs. Corey was presented to the princess the party had been going for some time and in attempting to curtsey Olga swayed. Then Princess Margaret swayed, then Olga swayed again . . . in the end the pair of them, clutching hands, went around the room like a whirligig, scattering guests and glasses. A memorable moment.

A tall head choirboy was once leading a glittering procession into the Cathedral. So taken was he with the majestic occasion that he held the ceremonial cross even higher than usual – and brought down an array of frayed flags and banners hanging heavy with dust. The flags came down onto the heads of the congregation.

The present Bishop, The Right Reverend Dr. David Stancliffe, was at the head of a later colourful column processing slowly down the aisle to the sound of celestial singing and came to a halt at the choir. Around his neck was hung a microphone so that his incantations could be heard throughout the great spaces of the Cathedral. Beside him, as an attendant, halted a slightly puzzled-looking choirboy and at a given moment in the crowded ceremony the Bishop took the heavy mitre from his head and carefully handed it to the boy. After more prayers and responses it was time to replace the high pointed head-dress and the bishop spoke out of the corner of his mouth to his young attendant. "Now the mitre is placed on the head". Nothing happened. The Bishop repeated the instruction then looked sideways at the choirboy *who had placed the mitre on his <u>own</u> head*. The microphone broadcast the Bishop's protest "Not on *yours* lad! Mine!"

A previous bishop led a diocesan party to the Vatican for an ecumenical meeting with the Pope. They were puzzled because His Holiness addressed them in German – he had been told they came not from Salisbury but Salzburg.

After a tradition going back eight centuries, Salisbury

Cathedral in the nineteen-nineties was the first to have young girls as part of its choir. Twenty girls joined the twenty boys in singing everything from hymns to (on occasions) happy-clappy mission songs. Although they never sang together in formal services they came up against historic opposition. They did not have the quality of the boys it was said. But in their bright emerald gowns they were certainly novel and definitely decorative. Soon every cathedral choir in the country had their singing girls. Now, in one part of their recorded repertoire, the choir performs a home-grown oratorio 'The Resurrection' written in The Close by composer Simon McEnery with the libretto by Canon Jeremy Davies, the Cathedral Precentor. It was commissioned by the late David Cooke and his wife Anne, who were our neighbours when we lived in The Walton Canonry.

One of the leaders in the campaign to bring in girl choristers was Mary Archer, wife of Jeffrey, the novelist. My wife Diana organised the raffle. Mary Archer does not normally do things by halves and she gave herself to the cause in a good many ways. She has a good singing voice herself and she produced a compact disc of Christmas Carols, with a backing, of course, of female voices. We still play ours at Christmas.

Some people did not like the then Mrs. Archer's forthrightness. There is a story that, in the course and cause of recruiting support, she travelled to the West Country where she was asked to stay overnight in the house of a local lady. She agreed, presumably as it would save the campaign a hotel bill. The problem was that the hostess was so excited at the prospect of a famous guest that she organised a dinner party of her friends so they could all meet her. But the visitor thought otherwise.

Soon after she arrived Mary Archer announced that she had gone through a busy day and was going to bed.

And she did so. She did not appear again, leaving the dinner guests to chat in whispers among themselves.

⁓

Ten years after the establishment of girl choirs at British cathedrals, a celebration was held at Salisbury. It was on a Saturday – at the end of the week of his second high profile trial when Jeffrey Archer had been convicted and was awaiting sentence on the following Monday. Every seat was taken in the nave – except two at the front. Everyone knew who was meant to sit in those seats and the betting was heavily against anyone turning up to claim them. But the doubters were wrong. Five minutes before the emerald girls came singing down the aisle their champion, by this time *Lady* Archer, appeared with another lady and sedately took her place.

After the celebration service there were drinks and a supper for the adults while the girl choristers showed that they could eat as well as sing. At the drinks reception both Diana and I were a little surprised that Lady Archer appeared to be standing alone. People were probably not shunning her, but they were keeping a certain distance, so we went to converse with her. We had both met her previously but after a few pleasantries we had run out of things to say to a lady whose husband was almost certainly going to prison the following Monday. So I said to her: "You've just had an interesting week."

"Not so interesting as next," she said.

She had just published a book, a scientific treatise, and I mentioned I had seen some of the favourable reviews. "And all this publicity," she said with a shrug. "Has not done it any harm at all."

When John Major was Prime Minister he invited the Salisbury Cathedral choir, or a section of it, to sing Christmas carols at Number Ten, Downing Street. A selection of the singers travelled there in their mini-bus and they were a great success with the guests.

It was during one of these evenings that Jeffrey Archer appeared and invited them to repeat the performance at his penthouse overlooking the Thames. An adult member of the choir said to me: "We turned up at his place and he opened the door. It was full of people and he let us in. Then he told us to take our shoes off to protect his carpet".

CHAPTER 24

Set in Stone

THERE IS NO SADDER, NO more frustrated man in the world than the monumental mason who cannot spell. You see their heartbreaking efforts to correct their dyslexia on tombstones all over the country. Sometimes they give up. There is a grave at Stanwell which incisively records that the occupant died on February 30th – a bonus day on earth or another day in Paradise?

Edward Hardwick's commemorative black slab in the Cathedral at Salisbury is also a memento to the mason who carved it. He missed the 'h' in 'Cathedral' and then made it more obvious by attempting to erase it somehow and only compounding the error. There is a visible hollow where in his anguish he tried to rub it out. In the end he gave up and tightly inserted the missing letter above the word with an arrow, perhaps unnecessarily pointing to his clumsy editing. His confidence shaken, he then committed another error on the next line carving "Residentiary" correctly until he achieved the last chip. He appears to have tried to eliminate a letter "i" only to replace it with two others. The poor man must have been shot to pieces by the time he let a "y" creep into the word "obit" because he made no attempt to alter it. It stares at you defiantly now after three hundred years. But the stone still remains, perhaps attracting more attention to the deceased Edward Hardwick than he would have otherwise merited. Perhaps, too, the upset family was given a cut price.

There is another puzzle on the stone of Thomas Lambert underfoot in the North Quire but this time it was no fault of the mason but of the government. It relates that Thomas died some months before his birth. "Borne May 13 Anno Domini 1683 and dyed Feb. 19 the same year."

Those were the days when calendars became chaotic because New Year's Day was fixed at March 25th – nine months before Christmas Day. This concludes that Jesus was a normal baby obeying human biological rules. But this put May 13 only eight months before the next February and thus in the same year.

Perhaps if only to save a crisis of confusion, the calendar was adjusted. Otherwise no one would have known when they were born – or when to die.

❦

Given the hindsight of seven hundred and fifty years, anyone wishing to be commemorated in the Cathedral should choose a plaque or stone, always providing the mason can chip in English. Busts and statues are not so sustainable. They become sadly worn, noses are knocked off and if the inscription is detached and goes missing no one knows who you are. The remnants of Sir Edward Heath are below the floor, so close to his Sunday seat that in different circumstances he could have heard himself sing. There are ancient but legible names and dates on flagstones in the frequently trodden Cloisters and preserved in private corners. The glass spindle of Rex Whistler will be giving its novel moving picture show for many years.

But the cab-ranks of old tombs drawn up on both sides of the nave by the heavy eighteenth century touch of James Wyatt have not fared well. They were probably in a poor state when he ordered their move and this was accomplished so haphazardly that the tombs and their occupants were often parted and scattered, never to meet again. Now visitors give them a rub, scrape them, even pat them as though they were some ancestor, and their stone features have been flattened. Few of them would recognise themselves. They also form twin barriers so that anyone wishing to reach the inner seats of the nave has to make a detour which takes some time if there is a moving crowd. It does not worry everyone. I remember seeing a local lady, not young and not apparently very athletic, lose patience in her attempts to reach a friend and launch herself over a tomb like a high jumper rolling over an Olympic bar, sliding deftly down the other side of the old effigy which continued to stare ahead.

There are tombs and likenesses of course, which are

exceptions. It would be a dull soul who could study the two people lying side by side as they so often did in life – Sir Richard Mompesson and his wife Dame Katherine. He is wearing brightly decorated armour and she has a black and gold dress with dainty shoes. They were repainted in 1964 and what an intricate and satisfying task that must have been. Perfectly at ease they are, but facing the wrong way. Traditionally such tombs face to the west but Sir Richard and his wife face east. In death they had to move to accommodate the new grand organ in 1877. And there is another curiosity: the large black marble tablet over them remains blank as if there was nothing more left to say. Their lasting and most elegant memorial, though, built by their descendants in 1701 is the airy and elegant Mompesson House on Choristers' Green in The Close, the perfect Queen Anne town house, so large and yet so light it looks as though it could fly.

One family, the Townsends, occupied the house for almost a hundred years. Its interior is a pattern of plasterwork. Sun flows through the wide windows into rooms in which eighteenth century people would feel at home. It has a nice enclosed garden and in one corner there is a tea house where you can buy refreshments including cream buns, provided by The National Trust.

⁂

Some people seem to be more appropriate, more comfortable perhaps, on their memorials when they are alone. One of the most touching and beautiful tombs in the Cathedral shows a devout lady in Jacobean dress, solitary and kneeling in everlasting prayer. She is Elihoner Sadler who worshipped in the pew below her monument for fifty years. She seems stern but with a self-contained sense of peace. On each side of her are placed the coats of arms of her two husbands, whom she outlived in her eighty years.

There is another memorial to twenty-eight people, in the main rich Americans and Canadians, who died when their express train crossed – or rather failed to cross Fisherton Bridge, Salisbury. It may have been racing to break the record for the time to London. It was 1st July, 1906, when trans-Atlantic liners called at Plymouth to cut a day off the sailing time to Southampton. Even in those days people seemed in a hurry. There were two express boat trains that connected with the incoming liners at Plymouth, one operated through Bristol and on to Paddington by the Great Western Railway and the other to Waterloo via Salisbury and run by the London and South-Western Railway.

In the early hours of 30th June, passengers came ashore from the ship 'United States' and went aboard the South-Western Train. Few had been to bed, it had been a good-natured night, and bets had been struck on the timing of the train to London. Passengers often wagered on train times when every company was stretching itself to better these. There were even rumours that passengers sometimes bribed the drivers to take risks.

The boat train gathered speed after Templecombe in Somerset; most of the 43 passengers were in their private compartments, talking over a late drink or dozing as the locomotive plunged through the summer night. Although he was experienced, the driver, William Robins, had never been through Salisbury Station non-stop. His train should have been below 30 miles per hour but it roared between the platforms at nearer 70. It failed to take the difficult curve beyond the station and came off the track hitting a local milk train. Some of the carriages of the express ended up hanging over the bridge into Fisherton Street. One body was found in a garden. Salisbury Hospital was only a few hundred yards away and some of the injured walked there, supported by local people in their night clothes.

The passengers who died, including five of one family called Sentell, are commemorated on the memorial in the Cathedral; Theodore Roosevelt, the United States President, sent a letter thanking Salisbury people for the help they gave that night. It was the worse train accident to have happened in railway history up to that time. The widow of one of the victims, a Mrs. Brodt of New York, whose then husband John E. McDonald (she had quickly remarried) died in the crash sued the London and South-Western Railway for $100,000 and received $35,000. In those days no railway engines had speedometers in their cabs. But the limit for trains going through Salisbury was reduced to 15 miles an hour.

From the earliest days there had always been disputes, struggles and suspicions in and around Salisbury about the coming of the railways. The Salisbury and Yeovil Railway Company, after fifteen years of frustration, finally took the plunge to start building with £4.2s.4d. in its bank account. Cottages grew about the first station, part of it designed by the great top-hatted Isambard Kingdom Brunel, and can still be seen today.

But there was an even earlier rail accident than the boat

train crash of 1906. Years before, a local train carrying cattle and sheep came off the line and ended up hitting the ladies' waiting room at Salisbury Station. Hysterical women were trapped in the building with anguished cows cavorting outside. The station was illuminated by gaslight and this had to be turned off to prevent an explosion (panic stricken cows are very explosive). So the rescue attempts had to be aided by lantern light and by *candles*. They were carried from local homes and shops and some were brought from the Cathedral on horseback. Hundreds of candles circled the truly Wagnerian scene. A train crash by candlelight! Two people were injured but the animals came off worse.

CHAPTER 25

For All The Saints

SALISBURY CATHEDRAL HAS BEEN REGARDED in diverse ways. Defoe thought being there was like being in a theatre; another more caustic view suggested that its space and height gave it the look of a mainline London station. Its contents, occupying its many corners and sly niches, could be likened to the stock of an outsized antique market. Even the stone carved figures displayed in sunlight across the width of the wonderful West Front have a "for sale" aspect. There are six ranks of them, more or less life sized, each standing with the patience of a saint, which most are. But they appeared to have voices also. Behind them is a wooden gallery, a suspended crate of choir boys who, on special occasions, sang uncannily. They called it The Sarum Rite. It has now been largely discontinued. The Bishop told me caustically: "Health & Safety."

It is a pleasant pastime of a summer day to sit on the grass outside the West Door and, with the help of a useful guide available at the Cathedral shop, pick out which of the carved figures is which. Many of them are Victorian, some are earlier, although they tend to wear out with wind and weather. Christ in Majesty is at the top, guarded above by the Eagle of St. John. Unnamed angels, (perhaps most angels are nameless) some with harps, some without, stand in the niches around. Then there is Moses struggling with the weight of the commandments, which most of us have done. Noah is there with his home-made boat and Daniel with his legendary lion. St. Peter has the keys and St. Paul a belligerent sword. St. Christopher carries the baby Jesus and St. George puts his foot firmly on the dragon. It was pleasant to think that St. Cecilia, the musical saint, smiled with pleasure when the choir sang behind its screen. There is a figure from Africa among the stony congregation, Canon Ezra, a priest and a scholar. In March 1991 he was killed in the crossfire between government forces and the Sudan People's Liberation Army. A modern Christian martyr, remembered now in English Wiltshire. On the lowest tier, next to the door as if ready to be of assistance to anyone, is the saint of Bemerton Village, George Herbert. They line up like a formidable football team.

～

Amazing things have happened in Salisbury, and on a regular basis (a lioness, escaped from a wild beast show, once attacked the horses of a local stage coach) and often surprising characters have coloured its history (a tramp called

Mr. Happy was once a witness at a murder trial).

But few personalities have aroused the comment and almost universal condemnation as James Wyatt who closed the Cathedral for three years while he rearranged the heritage of five centuries. In 1789 he shut the doors and got to work, especially on the silent traffic jam of interior tombs. He moved the last resort of the famous without favour. The tomb of one bishop was even "mislaid" according to the baffled records and never found again. Others were transported to their present-day positions, standing like cabs at a rank along the nave. Visitors who regard with awe the effigy of someone famous may well be revering an empty box or one containing the remains of several other worthy people. There was much confusion and some of the stony resting places may now only be occupied by spiders.

In his quest for light and straight lines Wyatt did not hesitate to remove the great Medieval windows over the West door and replace them with plain glass. The priceless wreckage was then brutally dumped in the Town Ditch and, as I have already related, was to be unearthed by a Close vicar, Stanley Baker, who offered some considerable remnants to the Dean and Chapter. They regrettably could find no use for them. Dejected he went away. So much for dedication.

Even today people speak of James Wyatt through clenched teeth. He was called the "perpetrator of a prolonged and hideous practical joke" and many other things, often to his face. He also had the bell tower pulled down. Feelings were more mixed about this. It had been built originally because the spire was too fragile to accommodate ringing bells but in drawings the tower does not appear unseemly, except in its conjunction with the Cathedral. Shops and alleys and houses had sprouted around it and it had desperately lapsed. Thomas Brown, the sexton, sold beer there at all hours, it was the dallying place of wicked women and two of the bells were cracked. The rest, apart from one, were sold. An advertisement for the remnants of the building appeared in March, 1790, in the 'Salisbury Journal' – "To be sold . . . the materials of a very large building . . ." One of the lumps of masonry now sits in the Salisbury garden of Martin Thomas, my dentist. He does not know how it got there.

Recently a team of television explorers discovered the remains of the bell tower – something hundreds of visitors do each year merely by looking down from the roof of the Cathedral. It is clearly outlined below the grass of The Close on a dry summer's day. The same investigators unearthed a human skeleton which was not surprising either. There are a lot of old bones where that came from – the original graveyard.

Wyatt, whatever ire he provoked, did a positive thing in tidying up the huge burial ground and grassed over the top which gives it the cricket field surface it has today. It also prevented the grazing cows falling into tombs as they had done for years. Some of the cows had belonged to choristers, given to them in the hope they would benefit from a supply of fresh milk. By some chance, in his clear-out of the shambling area, Wyatt also spared the one thing that should have been rescued in the bell tower. Among the beer and the bustles of the visiting women was what can only be called a contraption. It still looks like a contraption today – probably the oldest working clock in the world and also the oldest piece of working machinery. Put together in about 1386 the clock grunted and groaned in a corner of The Bell Tower, hardly noticed during the evenings of revelry. It was carted away before the demolition and was put into a grimy and dank corner of the main tower of the Cathedral and carried on uncomplainingly marking time until 1884 when it was moved aside altogether and a new clock was installed. It remained in the tower, unheeded, until 1928 when a man called Mr. Robinson saw it and wondered what it was. Mr. Robinson knew about clocks. He was a member of The British Horological Institute. He had never seen anything like this.

It is a story of long-term dedication. The clock, or its skeleton because it was hardly more, was taken down and transported twenty-five years later (during which time there was a war) to the works of Messrs. John Smith and Sons of Derby. There, after much intense study and delicate investigation, it was taken to pieces and put back together again so that the Medieval clocksmith who had built it would have nodded recognition and approval. Rolls-Royce, conveniently at Derby, helped with their x-ray equipment.

The moment of triumph arrived in July, 1956, when the same Mr. Robinson who had found the clock in the tower stood before a distinguished scientific audience and, in the most simple of ceremonies, re-started it. There was a collective holding of breath. He cut a ceremonial tape and the clock began to tick obediently. Clock-men are usually unfussy (which is why they like clocks). Mr. Robinson said modestly that it was "quite the most exciting thing I have seen in a long time."

The ancient timepiece stands today in the nave of the Cathedral looking odd for a clock. It has no hands and no dial. It looks something like the engine of an early flying machine. But it phlegmatically keeps its measure which is sounded by chimes through The Close. A triumph for a modest man called Mr. Robinson who enjoyed the wonders of time.

CHAPTER 26

Faces from the Past

PEOPLE TODAY CAN ONLY IMAGINE what the inhabitants of Salisbury looked like seven hundred years ago. But our curiosity can be partially satisfied by the clues left by the deft stonemasons who carved the many faces to be seen in the Cathedral. Who, for example, is the jovial man with the squashed hat who laughs (or smirks perhaps) in the Trinity Chapel? He is a figure of fun and yet there is more than a touch of sadness, even desperation, about him. He reminds me of Sir Laurence Olivier as Archie Rice in John Osborne's play 'The Entertainer'. Then in the South Quire Aisle is a belligerent monkey about to hurl a nut at anyone who gets too close. Perhaps the signature of a mason who was nicknamed Monkey by his workmates. Perhaps known for flinging bits of stone.

These chippy craftsmen quietly enjoyed leaving puzzles for posterity. In the Chapter House, for some the most welcoming part of the Cathedral is a head with three faces. One looks forward, a second to the left and a third to the right, like a French detective glancing around him with gallic suspicion. More thoughtful viewers think it represents the Holy Trinity. Others believe that the mason, short of a subject and with an area of wall to fill simply carved a self portrait – a study of himself from three aspects.

These thirteenth-century mallet and chisel men seem to have been under no particular instruction for much of their work. It is almost as if the master-mason thought about it on a Monday morning and decided: "Let's have a go at Sodom and Gomorrah this week." And they began to chip. This is why the faces in the friezes that surround the Chapter House are more than probably the features of known townspeople in long-ago Salisbury. They were given an open canvas and told to read – and depict – the first two books of The Bible, Genesis and Exodus, with a local cast.

So today we can stand engrossed in this huge, calm eight-sided room and follow the story like a comic strip. Perhaps the Bishop, the Dean and the Precentor, who presided here over discussions about Cathedral business and listened to the reading of a chapter from The Bible (which is why it is called The Chapter House), might have let their attentions stray momentarily to the Old Testament cartoon around them.

We see God busily creating the earth, the sky, the sun and the moon, as well as various plants and animals and, of course, gilding then spoiling the lily, with human beings. We see Adam and the nagging Eve, plus the serpent, muttering inducements. Cain invents murder and Noah, with one eye on the rain clouds, gets working on his boat; Sodom and Gomorrah are reduced to ashes but Lot escapes with his wife who becomes a pillar of salt after defiantly looking back. Those early men had a lot of woman trouble. Contemporary errors are easily spotted; the Egyptians fatally attempt to cross the Red Sea on chariots not invented until centuries later and the Tower of Babel is built like an everyday English castle where the local nobility lived in those much later times.

Each face in this everlasting serial is quaintly and carefully fashioned. These faces could be seen in everyday Salisbury, in the streets, in the market place; Adam could have been the baker and Eve the baker's wife, known to be difficult with shoplifters. Noah might have been recognised from his surrounding carpenter's shop and Abraham from the his next door mason's yard. It must have been fun and it varied a day chipping at stone. God is represented undoubtedly as someone held in high regard. Someone like the mayor or the money-lender.

Over the eight-sided building, you can hardly describe it as a mere room, floats - yes floats – a celestial fan-vault ceiling. Around the horseshoe of the walls are the seats of the canons who, while a chapter from the Old Testament is read aloud, could, by lifting their eyes, see it illustrated in the carved figures above them.

The Chapter House has the gift of silence, a silence that seems to have been built into it by those early men. It is like a huge but comfortable library, housing an important book – Magna Carta, one of the treasures of civilisation. But, on occasions, the surrounding space can readily become animated, lively and warm. Sometimes a bar is installed and the great space will shrink with the get-together of drinkers and talkers. I have seen people leaning, even sitting, on the worn and hoary Penny Table where it is said the original builders impatiently queued for their money every pay day.

One evening last year, a group of jolly teenagers, black boys and girls from a South African township, sang and danced there. They came to perform with the choir and the local Choral Society in the Cathedral. During the interval I was making my way in the direction of the Chapter House where refreshments beckoned, when I saw the Bishop, David Stancliffe, in mufti, sitting alone in a remote and empty row. I asked him if he were going for a drink. He replied: "I was waiting for someone to invite me."

Although I was not directly involved with the event, any more than he was (except it was his Cathedral) I took it upon myself to take the lead towards the red and white wines. At the door of the Chapter House it became apparent that the African entertainment was continuing. The mass of teenagers were still singing and swaying to a tribal chorus. Somehow my Lord Bishop and I took a wrong way and found ourselves trapped behind a chorus line of black girls all wobbling and waving their splendid backsides as they sang. We were hemmed in. The Bishop said solemnly: "I don't think I should be here."

He performed a smart manoeuvre and deftly escaped. I followed.

Magna Carta, the root of the laws of England and most of the world, is not as you might imagine a Great Charter would be. For a start, there is nothing very bulky or official about it. Before I ever saw it I believed it would be encased in several bound volumes with references to such things as "Section B (a) subsection N. Taking fish from ponds" or "Late payment of rents" or "See Appendix XXI. Allowable width of ploughshares". But nothing of the sort. What confronts you standing before its commonplace display cabinet is a single sheet of about 3,000 words, the length of a short story. But it is a work of minute and painstaking art on an oblong of vellum, each character of ancient English like an illustration. There were thirteen or possibly more copies made and four survive today, each one different. Apparently the scribes made no corrections, nor detectable spelling errors.

There is a nineteenth century bronze in Salisbury Cathedral which succinctly tells the story of how Magna Carta came about. The bronze originates in Paris but they have got the story right. King John of England, looking bad-tempered with a touch of the furtive, sits beside his adviser Archbishop Langton who is plainly pointing to the document on the royal lap with the clear instruction: "Sign this or there's going to be trouble."

The trouble is clearly present, a knight at the King's other hip with a sword drawn.

King John, by the fanciful illustrations of the thirteenth century is depicted as something of a spoiled fop. There is one where he is being offered the gift of a chalice and looking sulky as if he expected something more. He stands against a pillar, with one black-stockinged leg bent like someone hanging about at a corner. But his failings were not entirely personal. He believed in waging unwinnable wars and alienating his own subjects by forcing them to pay for them, in both lives and cash, a sad story that has echoes even today. Nobody liked the King from the top ranking barons, through the middle classes, the squires and landowners, down to the seething people who dragged their lives out in mud and dust to make a groat. The barons cornered the King at Runnymede on the Thames. The venue was chosen so that King John would not have time to wriggle out during the short journey from his Windsor home. The barons were encamped a comparative distance to the west. On a Monday morning in June they came face to face. The King, faced with swords and no-nonsense faces, signed.

Salisbury has its Magna Carta today because of the man behind the building of the great Cathedral that now stands like a guardian around it. Elias de Dereham, the driving force behind the building, was years previously secretary to Stephen Langton, Archbishop of Canterbury, and it was he who looked over King John's shoulder by the river Thames as the monarch, doubtless with a resigned sigh, pressed the royal seal at the foot of the document. The King apparently could not write more than a few words which included his name, although it is said he could read "to an extent".

Elias was given ten copies of the Charter, each written by

a different clerk at a painstaking rate, and when he returned to Salisbury and his dream of building the great Cathedral he brought one with him.

Elias never ceased his endeavours. He was accused of siding with the barons, the Pope was suspicious of him and he was exiled. But he was never beaten and lived to see the Cathedral rising every day before his eyes, and in the knowledge that Magna Carta was in his keeping. It is all the more extraordinary that among the memorials of forgotten people, among the florid tombs and the posing statues of the anonymous, there was never any room for the likeness of Elias de Dereham until after the Second World War. The statue erected then near the south transept is very obviously not from the distant past but it is a figure with a vibrant face, an image with which he might well have been pleased. He looks like he might well be surveying the surroundings wondering about possible improvements.

As for Magna Carta, if the truth be told its display in the Chapter House is scarcely worthy of it. Changes are in the offing, even a Magna Carta Centre has been discussed. The small document that changed the world

CHAPTER 27

What happened to Magna Carta?

ALL THE WRITTEN HISTORY THAT survives regarding the vast and mysterious Cathedral is gathered on shelves and in locked cabinets (for it has not always been safe) in the Library found on top of thirty-seven ancient steps. It is a place full of words, documents, promises, truths and downright lies. The steps are tight – one person wide – spiralling around a stone column. They have been trodden so long, centuries, that whole pieces have worn away and have had to be replaced with insets of stone. And now the inserted stones are also wearing. They lead to a small pointed door which takes you into a long room redolent with the scent of leather and wood.

There are two ranks of warm-looking bookshelves, an air of assured quietness and a clock that ticks with the soft insistence peculiar to library clocks. On one of the shelves are three eighteenth century books containing the remains of mice squashed cruelly in between the pages by cathedral choirboys, bored with singing praises.

This is the domain of Suzanne Eward and has been for more than thirty years. She has spent her life sorting through precious books, tending them and often being their first reader in centuries. She is a small, calm woman with an eye for a story, and you suspect a deep sense of humour. She wears the Cathedral emblem brooch. When she arrived at the library (she is also custodian of the archives and the munument room – munument pronounced with a first syllable like munitions). It is there that the most ancient and most precious remnants of the Cathedral history are kept. But not all of them. I asked if they still had the relic of the Virgin Mary found at the apex of the spire. Was it under lock and key? "It's right here!" she said briskly, walking a few feet to a window ledge and producing a lead canister about the size of a large tea cup. There it was. You could pick it up. Unfortunately whatever it contained, a piece of cloth from the Virgin's raiment, it is supposed, was long gone. Dealers in relics apparently used to ride the length of Christendom on donkeys , not so long ago.

The Close Constable's handcuffs and coshes from Napoleonic times are also in Suzanne Eward's custody. "At one time," she said looking about her. "This place was in a very poor state. Beetles had almost eaten away the floor, the bookcases collapsed into piles and irreplaceable books were taken from the shelves, and never returned."

It was no place to keep Magna Carta. But there it was kept, one of the most precious documents in the world, among the sagging bookcases, falling down with their weight of leather-bound wisdom. There were files on everything from receipts for choirboys' socks to invoices for incense. There were everyday letters, brief and to the point (a complaint that only one member of the clergy had been available to take the Sacrament service one Sunday and that he mumbled) and the lengthy proceedings of Cathedral councils, livened by the occasional, often scurrilous, court case.

In the time that the library and its relics were being rescued, Suzanne Eward took herself off to Wells Cathedral where she sat down quietly and catalogued its collection of books – those published before seventeen hundred. By the time, in the nineteen eighties, she had returned to Salisbury, the new library was equipped with fine bookcases. They stand straight as soldiers now, each with its own finial. They are made from elm glowing in the veils of spring sunshine falling through the window. The wood had arrived as if by a miracle. Dutch Elm Disease had struck the sturdy trees in The Close. They were sadly standing, dying giants, and had to be felled. But their wood was used in the bookcases truly fashioned by the Cathedral carpenters. Keeping to the tradition of local craftsmen throughout the centuries these men have left a trace of themselves behind. Below one of the finials above the shelves is a list of the names of the workmen who carved the new library.

Today, lodged alongside manuscripts from as far back as the ninth century, are the three books which never lose their interest for visitors. Two are volumes of Cicero's writings which, when opened reveal that they are the final resting place of the unfortunate Cathedral mice, captured by choirboys. By now, after close on three centuries, they are hardly more than mouse-shaped splodges. One had an epitaph in a boyish hand. "The first mouse we killed."

The prize exhibit of this grotesque exhibition is a 1684 edition of Suetonius Tranquillus (page 640). A very large mouse indeed is spread-eagled in this page, pressed like a purple flower. And tranquil indeed. From the ancient window there you can look out over the green Cloisters garden with its two spreading Cedar of Lebanon trees. Once there were three, but one has disappeared; another is quite modest, but the main tree spreads itself gloriously over the lawn. "They were planted for the accession of Queen Victoria in 1837." said Suzanne. "We still have the receipt." She produced it in no time. (What a filing system!) Dated 22 December, 1836, the receipt is for "Three fine Cedars of Lebanon". Thomas Moody did not have to wait long for settlement. On 1st February, 1837, he was paid. The cost of the sumptuous tree that outstretches over the Cloisters garden was £3.18s. – with planting.

But the strangest story to come from this place so full of tales concerns Magna Carta itself. At the time when the archives were falling in on themselves and the books were holding up the bookcases, Magna Carta was precariously housed in the room. Mindful of the valuable editions that regularly disappeared from the crumbling shelves, the then custodian, Dr. Elsie Smith, became so worried about the priceless document that she took matters into her own hands.

Each night she would take Magna Carta home with her. *And put it for safety under her bed!*

CHAPTER 28

Summer on the Hill

old Sarum

MEANWHILE, OUT ON THE NORTHERN reaches of this story, Old Sarum lurks in serenity. It is as if time has gone on so long that it does not care any more. But today people are again going there, climbing the poached-egg hill, taking in the scenery and the history. It still rises on most days, remote and cold to the eye, letting the world come to it, or not, as it pleases; a take it or not attitude. You can almost sense it shrugging its old shoulders. Every cloudy sky, every wisp of wind, even in summer, draws a veil across it. But we went there again, on a morning of Maytime warmth, the old stones glowing a little, trees full, the hill drenched with buttercups. From the top you could see the meadows of England spread out like a skirt.

Our grand-daughter Zoë known, despite her Cathedral

Christening, as Beany, began picking the buttercups but gave up. "Too many to do," she said. But with the energy of a child going on three she did a quick barrack-room check of the soldiers' quarters. The still hefty walls which had known the oaths and jokes of the Norman conscripts resounded with the excitement of a child.

The views from the top remain unchanging. A house may be built in the distance, a road casually appears between the trees; they have put in a car-park and a hut where you can buy toy Norman swords, but little has altered in the panorama. Nearly eight centuries on, the spire of the Cathedral, built to trump Old Sarum, is still clear, but misty and afar as if, wisely knowing its place

Both Constable and Turner, in almost unique agreement, saw Old Sarum as a wildly angry place. Constable was able to indulge uncriticised in his favourite unkempt sky and Turner brought his own personal storm. Each of the rivals made the small mountain take on the aspect of a battered sea-coast, a headland facing up to a storm, an island besieged by the ocean.

The distant views give way to the reality that a change in the weather gives a sweep of bright inland green. Water, or lack of it, was a problem throughout history demonstrated now by a sulky eye at the bottom of a well – 230 feet down.

English Heritage has done its best to make Old Sarum welcoming. You can telephone the little hut-cum-shop they have set there and a bright twentieth century voice answers: "This is Old Sarum Castle – Naomi speaking." The original cathedral is still happily obvious, or its outline at least, laid out with poetic geometry below the castle ramparts. The priests of old would find it particularly draughty now. As the years went on its walls diminished like the frame of a man growing elderly. The hewn stones, and those from the decaying castle, were lifted to Salisbury where they have spent a useful second life in the wall around the Close, in the sturdy gateways and in the houses within, some still bearing the initials and carvings of masons who hoped that at least and at last posterity might notice them.

Old Sarum became ghostily abandoned. Pepys confessed that he would be "affrighted to be there alone at night." His fear might have been echoed by soldiers posted at the top during the Second World War, despite the presence of three large anti-aircraft guns. What good is an A.A. gun against a ghost?

Henry of Avranches poetically, if misleadingly, described Old Sarum: "The city is stood in the castle and the castle in the city." It's a neat image but inaccurate since in his 13th century day most of the remaining habitations were outside the castle walls. The place was burdened over the years with the normal lot of such outlandish locations. It served time as a prison, although some prisoners clambered to freedom. People were sometimes willing to hide them, with certainly more enthusiasm than the lepers who sometimes wandered from the colony that was once established there. Stones were later carted off to Salisbury where they formed the walls of the new two-storey prison at Fisherton, and penned in the lepers who were later callously brought into the city – to reside, needless to say, beside the town drain.

But the most notable part that Old Sarum came to play in later history was to be the scene of an infamous famous fraud.

Down the summertime green slope from the fallen castle keep there was once an elm called The Parliament Tree and below its leaves was conducted, at each election time, a solemn mockery. For Old Sarum was one of the notorious Rotten Boroughs which sent politicians to Parliament without even the excuse of a vote. Old Sarum found itself with seven voters and one candidate. An awning was erected beside the tree and the ritual performed with straight faces. For more than a century members were likely to be sent to Westminster on that basis. Sometimes they got the right man, Pitt the Elder was one. It was hardly democratic and not popular (although there was a fair faction for it). Cobbett, on his 'Rural Ride', could not even face going to the "accursed hill" of Old Sarum. But after the bitterly contested Reform Act of 1830 there were no more single-sided elections, no more favours given and received by people in high places.

In 1905 the Parliament Tree fell down, perhaps from lack of use. In recent times another tree was planted by Robert Key, Salisbury's M.P. but, in his own words, "seems to have languished."

One dark night some thieves climbed from the road and painstakingly prised the plaque which the present Member had unveiled on the spot. They got the bolts from the wall and lowered the tablet to the ground. And there it was found the following morning. Perhaps it had proved too heavy to remove. It was carried to St. Lawrence's Church in nearby Stratford-sub-Castle and given a temporary home. Among his many other responsibilities, St. Lawrence is the patron saint of languid and lazy people. (There is an old London expression for someone who is weary – "He is suffering from Lawrence".) So perhaps the thieves were too lazy to take their loot away. Or could it be that up there in the night they saw or heard the Norman ghosts and, like Pepys, became "affrighted" and made off down the dark hill leaving their loot behind?

CHAPTER 29

A View to the Past

THERE IS A PAY DESK the everyday entrance to the Cathedral. The entrance fee is nominal but it is pointedly suggested that £5 for an adult is appropriate. Some visitors refuse to pay and are admitted anyway. I once heard a young student protest, "But I just want to look around. I don't want to pray or anything." A look-around can take an hour, a day, an entire holiday or a lifetime. Not everyone has seen every corner, has solved every secret, has considered every mystery.

Then, suddenly it seems, you can see there is another aspect. Climb to the top of the tower, with the spire above you, pointing to the sky. From there on a good day you can see what seems to be half of England. You can certainly look north for one and a half miles and see the shape of the hill at Old Sarum.

Author's Thanks

WHEN THEY FIRST KNEW THAT I was writing 'Almost
Heaven, Tales About a Cathedral', some people in
Salisbury feared it might be some sort of exposé, a scurrilous
story full of items that have been best forgotten and are
certainly rarely mentioned.

It might be possible to write such a story – but this is not
it. There are included some quite astonishing tales, but where
I have thought the appendage of names would cause harm or
embarrassment I have left them out. In one case I have deleted
an elderly lady's age.

Many people have helped me. Indeed it was amazing how
residents of The Close and wider places have come forward
to offer a funny story or a strange occurrence. I have
acknowledged library sources but, in particular, I would like

to thank the following for their help:

Stephen and Kate Abbott, Alison Pinkerton, Tim Hatton, The Rev. Jeremy and Angela Ames, Priscilla Tapley, Patricia Cave-Smith, Peter Smith, Suzanne Eward, Sarah Stancliffe, Christopher Tunnard, Tricia and Chris Dragonetti, Julian Wiltshire, Ruth Newman, Robert Key M.P., Jennifer Bowen, Daphne Scamell, Dr. Frank Collings, John Cox, Lily Laker, Frank Lockyer, Eleanor Eckett, Tony Markham, Martin Thomas, George and Jane Apter, Helen Russell, Kevin Oborne and Leonie Cobey. Members of my own family: Lois Faulkner, my grandson Joe Faulkner, Alexandra Thomas, Mark Thomas and Diana Thomas, my wife and constant help, Mr. Elwood of Elwood Books, Salisbury, the name by which we always know him – although he says his business is named after Elwood, his late cat.

Bibliography

Endless Street. *John Chandler.* 1983

Sarum Close. *Dora Robertson.* 1938

Salisbury. The Houses of the Close. *Royal Commission on the Historical Monuments of England* 1993

Salisbury Past. *Ruth Newman and Jane Howells.* 2001

Salisbury. The History of an English Cathedral City. *David Durnett.* 1978

Salisbury Cathedral Close Guide. *Roger Croft.* 1997

Ancient and Historical Monuments in the City of Salisbury. Vol 1. *Royal Commission on the Historical Monuments (England)* 1980

Mississippi Memoir. *James Leroy Tapley* 2007

The Salisbury Avon. *Ernest Walls.* 1929

The Harnham Water Meadows. *Hadrian Cook, Michael Cowan, Tim Tatton Brown.* 2006

The Quiet Waters By. *Aylmer Tryon.* 1988

Cathedral Cats. *Richard Surman.* 1993

Thomas Hardy – The Time-Torn Man. *Clair Tomlin.* 2006

Letters To My Mother. *Helen Foley.* 1992

Journeyman. *Walter Partridge.* 1991

Buildings of England. Sir Nikolaus Pevsner. 1972

John Constable and The Fishers. *R. B. Beckett.* 1952

Henry Fielding. *Pat Rogers.* 1979

The Course of My Life. *Edward Heath.* 1998

The Great Salisbury Train Disaster. *Jeremy B. Moody and George Fleming*